LET THE CHURCH SAY AMEN TO STEM

GUIDEBOOK TO LAUNCHING AND GROWING EXTRAORDINARY YOUTH PROGRAMS

Natalie S. King

Foreword by Rose M. Pringle

I AM STEM, LLC
Atlanta, GA

LET THE CHURCH SAY AMEN TO STEM

Published by I AM STEM, LLC *in partnership with* The Literary Revolutionary.

www.theliteraryrevolutionary.com

ISBN #: 978-1-950279-07-4

Edited + Formatted by The Literary Revolutionary + Team

Cover Design By: Nikola Nikolic and Natasha Jackson

Manufactured in the United States of America

Follow the Author!
Twitter and Instagram: @DrNatalieKing
www.drnatalieking.com

LET THE CHURCH SAY AMEN TO STEM

GUIDEBOOK TO LAUNCHING AND GROWING EXTRAORDINARY YOUTH PROGRAMS

Jack and Mary-Alice,

It was a pleasure meeting you at the GSU Return to Learn event.

Thank you for attending so that I could meet you in person. I appreciate you for also sharing your book with me.

Look forward to reading this summer!

Natalie King

This book is dedicated to all pastors, youth leaders, educational directors, and those who are interested in enacting change within your communities! I have specifically written this book for ambassadors for Christ and ordinary people who seek to carry out God's extraordinary plan for your lives.

Tony, Antonio, and Angelo, this is for you!

Do not go where the path may lead, go instead where there is no path and leave a trail. **– Ralph Waldo Emerson**

As we have therefore opportunity, let us do good unto all men, especially unto them who are of the household of faith. **– Galatians 6:10**

CONTENTS

FOREWORD

In a tiny country district in Jamaica, my local pastor introduced me to the world of education. She was devoted to teaching youth the basics of arithmetic and reading in exciting ways. By the time I started primary school, I functioned at a third-grade level in reading and mathematics. Within the first week, I was promoted out of the first grade. My church literally provided me with the academic foundation that has shaped the trajectory of my life. Upon reflection, I realize that the seeds of success were planted and nurtured within a church culture that valued Christian living, educational achievement, and offered community support. While scriptural teaching prepared us for heaven, the educational achievement was encouraged as the route for social and economic mobility. The church was responsive, and through its socio-religious and educational programs, provided a bedrock of faith in training children in the way God intended for them to grow to become functional members of society.

The saying, "it takes a village" has not lost its meaning in the life of today's communities. Rather, it has become even more critical as society changes and is being driven by advances in science, technology, engineering, and mathematics (STEM). When we examine our communities, it is evident that many of our children are entering adulthood unprepared to be functional citizens. Schools and other educational institutions are failing to meet the diverse needs of our children; neither are they adequately preparing them in areas of study that include STEM. Furthermore, local, state, and national statistics clearly reveal deleterious educational disparities in general, with specific emphasis on the persistent underrepresentation of certain populations in STEM. Too often members of our church communities become trapped perpetuating the cycles of intergenerational poverty. Certainly, the church as one group of stakeholders, still has a foundational role to play in promoting educational excellence and social and economic development within communities. However, new approaches are now required. Daniel envisioned a time of great increase in knowledge, and I believe that we are currently living in that time. So, how should the church respond to the knowledge increase particularly related to STEM? What leverage does the church have in supporting STEM education within community-based ventures? Can church leaders develop effective educational programming within their communities?

For generations, churches have been given the authority and power to shape lives and thus the future of members of the community. Therefore, we must seek to create and maintain a 21st Century Christian culture that caters to the holistic development of our congregations and the communities that we serve. This includes preparing children to develop in ways that will allow them to take their rightful place, while positively contributing to the welfare of society. The conversation in John 21:17 and the charge given to Peter after declaring his love for Jesus was to "Feed my sheep."

This charge is still very pertinent today and I believe should be one of the stated missions of the church. As the good shepherd, Peter, was to provide the necessities for his sheep that would allow them to exist in the pastures. As church leaders, consider following the fearless example of my country town pastor by responding to the spiritual and secular (educational, socioemotional, and intellectual) needs of people in your care.

At a time when society is driven by advances in the STEM disciplines, with certain populations being excluded or marginalized, Dr. King's practical, hands-on guide provides you with resources and recommendations to extend and transform your place of worship to include a dynamic community for STEM learning. She infuses biblical principles with her own personal experiences so that it's genuine and meaningful. She candidly acknowledges the challenges and difficulties of engaging in this type of work, yet is hopeful about the results of rich partnerships that bridge the divide across institutions. This is timely! There is no doubt that the church's involvement in STEM learning has the potential to change the trajectory of demographics who have traditionally been excluded –such as children of color, children with disabilities, females, and those from low socioeconomic backgrounds. *LET THE CHURCH SAY AMEN TO STEM* contains cutting edge strategies for achieving the God-given charge to "feed my sheep."

Utilizing the wisdom and resources Dr. King provides, you too can create positive educational opportunities for STEM learning within and beyond the four walls of your edifice. This book allows you to examine your own specific contexts through reflections in order to design STEM programs in accordance with your community's needs. The church is certainly poised to bring sustainability and social justice to our nation through the development of educational programs consistent with the vision of the church as a light in dark places.

Rose M. Pringle, PhD
Associate Professor, Science Education
University of Florida

PROLOGUE
WHO AM I?

Who Am I?
A child, a student, a lady
I am 10 years old and try hard to accomplish my goals
I grew up in Queens
Eating hot dogs, hamburgers, and beans
I admired the weather each year
Spring, summer, fall, and snow everywhere
I have had heartache
Especially when my parents told us we would relocate
I did not want to leave my friends
These things I failed to comprehend
With broken hearts and tear-stung faces
We all headed to these new places
Palm Bay, University Park,
New friends, new faces, stone hearts
I am trying to cope as the years go by,
Soon I will be attending junior high
Things will get better, I know God cares
I will achieve my goals,
Someday, somehow, somewhere

As a 10-year old child, I wrote this original poem grappling with the question, "Who am I?" From that moment on, I have sought answers to this very question, redefining who I am - my purpose, passions, and dreams with each passing day. This poem was written while I was in a state of discontentment and despair as my family decided to relocate from Queens Village, New York to Palm Bay, Florida. I have fond memories of growing up in New York, although it was laced with tribulation and struggle. We rented the top floor of someone else's home - two adults and five small children occupying a one-bedroom one-bath pseudo apartment. Many people see the close relationship between my siblings and I and are often envious. Unbeknownst to them, the first years of our lives were spent sleeping head-toe on the same bed.

We experienced tremendous hardships, but at the center of our lives was our faith in God and our love for each other. Some of my happiest moments were spent in the house of the Lord. I vividly remember peering through the blinds on Sunday mornings, eagerly waiting to hear those two honks indicating that the church van was outside. I would seemingly fly down the stairs to accompany our landlord, Mrs. Graham, to church while Mommy got the younger children dressed. Whenever the weather was beautiful, I often walked to church with Mrs. Graham. If I were not in school, you would often find me in the house of the Lord or at a church-related function. I can recall my four siblings and I squeezing into my mother's Hyundai traveling across the New York boroughs for church rallies, conventions, and revivals. We went on outings with the youth group to places such as the Bronx Zoo, Dorney Park, Hershey Park, or Coney Island. My mother played cassette tapes of her favorite southern gospel songs from The Gaithers or Jimmy Swaggart, interspersed with Jamaican gospel by The Grace

Thrillers. We belted out every word; they seemed to be ingrained into our very souls. Mommy's favorite song was

> *Something beautiful, something good.*
> *All my confusion He understood.*
> *All I had to offer Him was brokenness and strife,*
> *But He made something beautiful of my life.*

I would not truly understand the profound meaning of these words until I got older and experienced a few life lessons of my own. Whether it was playing "Sword in Hand", competing to see who could find the bible verses first, learning how to do a simple two-beat on the drums, or falling asleep under a pew during a sermon that I was too young to comprehend; church was my second home. The practice of attending church and assembling myself with believers was instilled in me as a young child.

After we moved to Florida, I became even more involved during my tween and teen years by participating in bible quizzing, serving as the praise dance leader, and singing soprano on the praise and worship team. My mother oversaw vacation bible school, which we attended during the summer months. She also taught Sunday School and facilitated the Young Ladies Ministry. I grew up in the church and have served the Lord my entire life. Despite the mistakes I made along the way, I always found a way to recenter and get back on track, living life to the fullest with the heartiest of laughs that I inherited from my maternal grandmother.

In school, I became passionate about science and mathematics because these subjects bridged my natural inclination of being curious with my analytical way of thinking and making sense of the world. Two notable elementary school teachers tapped into my interests and giftedness in these subjects through their pedagogical approaches: Mrs. Paleta and Mr. Bihanna. My fifth-grade teacher, Mrs. Sherry Paleta, was full of energy and created ways to meaningfully engage her students in science. One particular activity that resonates with me is the owl pellet dissection to learn about the eating habits of birds. It was Mrs. Paleta's expectation that we asked questions, made predictions, and engaged in conversation and critical thought. She came to class with a sense of urgency each and every day, which produced an enthusiastic love for learning. Mrs. Paleta provided opportunities for us to explore the natural world around us. In the 6th grade, I had an excellent mathematics teacher, Mr. Bihanna. He typically lectured for about fifteen minutes where he called students to the whiteboard to work out problems and sat at his desk for the remaining class period as we practiced problems independently. If students needed scaffolding, he provided one-on-one assistance. If too many students asked the same question, he used it as a teachable moment for the class and returned to the whiteboard. Mr. Bihanna taught me not to fear math word problems, to trust the process, and struggle through them at my own pace to gain deep conceptual understandings.

What I loved most about Mr. Bihanna was that he always facilitated competitions on Fridays like "All Around the

World". I looked forward to opportunities to compete against my peers to measure the extent to which I mastered that week's content. Not only was I expected to be accurate in figuring out simple algebraic problems mentally, but I had to solve them with agility. I did not win every week, but I made it around the world enough times to internalize my brilliance in mathematics. Before starting middle school, I had realized my true passion for mathematics and science, although I still did not project myself into the image of a scientist or mathematician. In the seventh grade, I joined the international math team at Southwest Middle School sponsored by Mr. Lewis. I was the only Black student on the team with predominantly White and Asian males and I began to compete in local and statewide competitions surrounded by others who resembled my teammates. I did not consider myself to be the smartest team member, but I could solve basic arithmetic and convoluted word problems in my head within seconds, utilizing those same skills that I developed in Mr. Bihanna's class.

At church, my sisters and I participated in Bible quizzing where we memorized hundreds of verses each year and traveled across the state and nation competing. My ability to answer questions quickly and efficiently contributed to our success during the bible quizzing competitions. My church involvement resulted in academic success in school, while my school experiences promoted my effectiveness in church-related activities. There were many gray areas for me that could not be reduced to purely black or white. My identity and who I was at school was influenced by my Christian values, biblical teachings, and scriptures hidden in my heart; while my ability to learn and quote scriptures and answer higher order questions were mainly a result of my formal school experiences. As I grew older, I was perplexed and agitated because my love for the Lord and passion for mathematics and science never had an opportunity to unite in meaningful ways. I felt the need to neglect pieces of who I was to avoid disrupting the social norms of each setting.

Many of my peers in church struggled with science and mathematics. In fact, I learned that countless adults feared these subjects as well. I remember when a member of the prayer group, Minister Shirley Francis, asked Mommy who was a teacher at the time, to tutor her in mathematics. Minister Shirley was a middle-aged woman who was studying to pass a college algebra course that was a prerequisite for the nursing program. Acknowledging my talents, Mommy passed on the baton to me and recommended that I serve as her tutor. Not only did this provide me with an opportunity to put my mathematical skills to the test, but also it allowed me to earn a little pocket change during the process. I became nervous because the stakes seemed so high. Each week, I visited Minister Shirley's home, sat around her kitchen table talking her through how to solve problems while modeling the process and giving her opportunities to solve problems independently. Minister Shirley ended up passing the course and got accepted into the nursing program, which were great victories for her, but also a confidence booster for me. My ability to teach the content in such a way that someone else could master it, without formal training or educational degrees, revealed to me that I possessed a gift from God. I was unsure of how that gift would materialize and make room for me, but I gleaned in seeing a church sister succeed and reach new milestones in her career because I had the courage to say "yes".

It should come as no surprise that when I turned 16, my first job was cashiering at a local Winn-Dixie grocery store. I applied for the job and the store manager at the time, Mr. Casey, told me that he did not have any openings. I wrote a letter thanking him for giving me an opportunity to interview and hand delivered it to the store. Mr. Casey called me back into the store and explained that in his career as a manager, no one had ever written a "thank you" note after being denied employment. He noticed that something was different about me and offered the cashier position even though there were no available openings. I strove to be the most polite cashier, greeting all customers with a smile and friendly conversation. I was elated whenever my till was perfectly balanced matching the manager's figures to the penny!

In high school, I traveled thirty-five miles for the International Baccalaureate Program at Cocoa Beach High School. My older sister, Nicole, and I were determined to pursue medicine and open a practice together where I would serve children and she would be the primary care physician to their families. After all, becoming a pediatrician was the correct career path for someone who loved children and was proficient in science and mathematics, right? Even after I graduated with my bachelor's degree and taught high school science for three years, I was determined to pursue medicine and viewed my time in education as a form of service to the community prior to embarking on my lifelong career in medicine. Nicole and I are only one year apart, so I spent the first two decades of my life following her footsteps until God diverged me on my own path. After Nicole completed her undergraduate degree, she spent two years teaching high school science in Atlanta, GA prior to starting medical school. I was committed to teaching for a few years as well, but wanted to serve in the same city where I received my degree - Gainesville, FL.

I can share countless stories of my time in teaching. The lessons learned from those experiences are probably deserving of their own book. In retrospect, my approaches were liberal and unorthodox where I often chose to ask for forgiveness rather than permission to provide students with excellent learning opportunities even with the reality of having limited resources. They learned science in ways that were authentic and applicable to their lives. Imagine five or six electric skillets running with French toast, pancakes, eggs, bacon, and sausage! I used food to teach many of the core concepts in biology and chemistry. We learned the structure and functions of the four basic biological macromolecules, physical and chemical changes, human body systems (focusing on digestive and excretory), caloric intake, and so much more - all while making breakfast in the classroom. The students quickly realized the importance of bringing in an extension cord to plug the skillet with bacon outside so that when the smoke rose, it would not set off the fire alarm. I did not believe in teaching to the test, but rather focused my attention on students' mastery of the content to position them favorably to pass any test.

One memorable experience was when I entertained students' request to have their biology final exam at Disney's Animal Kingdom. I put the onus on the class to figure out how to navigate the bureaucratic channels to take the idea from conception to implementation. They spoke with the secretary to schedule a meeting with the principal and prepared a presentation and packet of information that contained the proposed activities. When the principal arrived in the classroom, he was greeted and escorted to his seat, which contained the proposal and light refreshments. The whole class took turns sharing how this field trip aligned with the standards. They outlined the culminating project that would result from this experience and provided a clear argument for why it would be beneficial. They were not only successful in getting permission but secured enough funds for the whole class to attend. While their peers were taking a traditional pencil/paper final, we were at "the happiest place on earth". My willingness to be receptive to the students' methods of resisting conventional schooling was what made me an effective educator. I believed in providing the highest quality learning experiences where students could make connections between the activities, learning goals, and their everyday lives.

Teaching presented its own challenges. Although I was young and Black, many students felt like they could not readily relate and that I was "born with a silver spoon in my mouth", as one of them so boldly declared. I remember teaching high school biology and chemistry, but always reserved time in the spring semester to show them how to write resumès, apply to colleges, and complete the free application for federal student aid (FAFSA). I ministered to children who endured great trauma, carried adult responsibilities, and were well on their way to becoming another statistic. Some were pushed through school without anyone saying, "I love you" or showing them through their actions. Many internalized that they were not good in science and had lofty goals of simply completing high school; college was an afterthought. Some students were already addicted to drugs and involved in gang-related activities, while others did not have a stable place to call home and rotated through shelters and distant relatives' apartments.

Although I could not relate to many of their stories, I saw how brilliant my young scholars were, and was determined to help them become a better version of themselves. I often reminisce about my humble beginnings and the many nights I cried myself to sleep praying that God would change my family's situation. Through my transparency and compassion, I reached many children before they could self-destruct. I chose not to ignore their silent cries for help or their desires to defeat intergenerational poverty. Many times, I closed my classroom door and encouraged students to look beyond their current conditions and use education and their faith in God as tools to rise above their circumstances. I held on to my faith and often invited students to church noting the importance of spiritual health in becoming holistically sound.

In retrospect, I have discerned that my life's experiences really do blur the lines between institutions. Yet, social conventions and societal norms have forced me to experience a disconnect between my love for the Lord and my passion for science. I wrestled to understand the true purpose of my life here in the earth realm, because science did not include the existence of God, and the sermons seemed to oppose or sometimes ignore the very presence of science. If I love science, does that mean that I am not a Christian or that I do not love God? My humble attempts to connect my two passions seemed to consistently fail as I embodied two oppositional forces like repelling magnets. As an adult, I continue to ask the same question, "Who am I?" to find my true identity as I toggle between institutions where corporate prayer is banned and ones where science is not openly welcomed.

Is there something wrong with me? Am I trying to connect two entities that were designed to be separate or are there some underlying truths and biblical principles that have allowed me to coexist in both spaces - staying true to my God without ignoring the reality of science? In this book, I share 8 biblical principles that have informed my journey. Each chapter includes several seeds of wisdom that provide deeper revelations into each principle. Allow these seeds to take root so that they can germinate and bring forth fruit to produce tangible results for children and families in your communities. At the end of each chapter are contemplative questions to help you delve deeper into the essence of each seed, and its applicability to your unique context. Engage with those questions individually and use them as discussion points for your church and community groups.

As a science educator, I am guided by the Framework for K-12 Science Education and the Next Generation Science Standards (NRC, 2012; NGSS Lead States, 2013) where students examine scientific phenomena as they deepen their understandings of crosscutting concepts, disciplinary core ideas, and science and engineering practices. There are eight science and engineering practices that represent behaviors of scientists and engineers as they investigate their natural world and design models, systems, and solutions. This book shares eight biblical "practices" presented in God's word that has informed my development of programming for youth. I hope that they will provide a strong foundation to launch and grow your own extraordinary community-based programs that will build the Kingdom of God.

I conclude by sharing my own personal testimony in the Epilogue - not about how I developed a STEM program, but how I was developed through the process of bringing the program to fruition. As a result of my obedience and willingness to be a vessel, countless children and their families have been impacted. God has shown me how to leverage community resources to start programming from the ground up. My hope is that you will apply these same principles to continue the great work within your churches and communities, so that young people can openly love science and God without feeling the need to choose.

Furthermore, our youth will have opportunities to engage with science in faith-based institutions thus broadening our understandings of the purpose of the Church and we can truly impact communities. I am in deep pursuit to fulfill my kingdom assignment in my career as an academic and science educator through community-based scholarship. This book is designed to spark conversation so that the people of God can broaden and transform their thinking. No more separation! No more operating in silos! No more excuses!

GETTING ON THE SAME PAGE

In the prelude, I shared select personal life experiences that inspired me to write this book. I want to also offer a few clarifications before we proceed to share what this book is NOT designed to do. This is not your typical guidebook providing a step-by-step linear process regarding the logistics behind starting youth programs. Procedures and policies vary between states, cities, and institutions. Therefore, I choose not to delve into the intricacies of those details. This book is birthed out of love so that we can get back to the basics. If you are already implementing programs, I hope that you can rethink how your programs and interventions are serving the community. If you do not currently offer outreach programs but desire to do so, this book provides insights into a few lessons that I have learned along the way. I highlight the nuts and bolts of some of the more elusive considerations that are often overlooked as you build and facilitate programs for youth and their families.

The title, *LET THE CHURCH SAY AMEN TO STEM*, is not meant to glorify science, technology, engineering or mathematics (STEM), but rather embrace these disciplines as tools to develop holistic youth programs. I refer to "the Church" as the body of Christ and not an edifice and understand that many churches may decide to collectively implement STEM programs for youth. These biblical principles are human-centered and acknowledge the humanity in the charitable work that we do as believers. When I say "AMEN", it insinuates an expression of assent or agreement. Typically, it is used to signal the culmination of a prayer. In some churches, saints may be moved to interject an "AMEN" while the pastor is preaching a sermon that speaks directly to their spirit or situation. Romans 14:11b states, every knee shall bow to me, and every tongue shall confess to God. I live by that scripture and am not worshipping the STEM disciplines by any means.

After deep reflection and prayer, God revealed the biblical principles that have undergirded my development and successful implementation of community-based STEM programs. I hope that these principles will provide a more useful, constructive, and accessible way for Christians to conceptualize possible roles to promote STEM education for youth. I do not intend to leave out or elevate one particular religion over another, but I am guided by my own personal experiences as a Christian and speak from that perspective. Even with the best of intentions, there will always be critics - which I welcome in hopes that we will break the silence and engage in conversations that go beyond Christian colloquialism. Let's not fear the ridicule or backlash of engaging in these types of discussions. We need more individuals who are led by the spirit of God in the STEM professions to spearhead innovations and lead with a sense of urgency and purpose. As the Church, we should encourage children to exercise their creativity and reconsider the types of programs and opportunities that we offer. Let us put aside denominational differences and come together to promote the greater good of communities in which we live and serve. Now that we are on the same page, let's embark on this journey together.

PRACTICE 1
CREATIVITY IS GOD'S SPECIALTY...
AND YOURS, TOO!

Genesis 1:1 - *In the beginning, God created the heaven and the earth.*

The first practice is derived from the very first verse in the Holy Bible, God's instructional book to the believers - creativity. The omnipresent, omniscient, and sovereign God existed before the universe was created. He has no predecessor, neither does He have a successor. There is no beginning or ending with God. He is the Master Creator and the eternally existent I am that I am. God spoke the heavens and earth into existence but then used nature to create. We must follow His example and see things spiritually before they can be manifested and brought to fruition. He proved Himself to be a problem solver and inventor. Before God

Everyone has the capacity to be creative.

was anything else, He was creative, and has provided us with raw materials to exercise our own creativity to solve local and global problems. We were made in His image and likeness, thus designed to create.

Darkness covered the face of the earth and God called light into being. First, He modeled how we should speak things into existence and not rely on our natural sight to determine what we can have or become. God also modeled what it means to envision those things that are not as though they were. God said that it was not good for man to be alone and created woman from Adam's rib. It is His will that we design solutions to problems, but it requires us to unlock our creative potential. The greatest creations are birthed from a need to solve a problem or desire to see something different and is usually preceded by failures. We must dare to imagine the possibilities of what our thoughts can become. This may require us to unlearn what we were taught in formal school...and even Sunday School.

God is not limited or intimidated by our formal degrees or training. People often think that God can't possibly use them because they are not intelligent enough, don't come from the "right" family, have made too many mistakes, do not have a college education, or attend a church with more pews than people. These are limitations or excuses that we place upon ourselves because God specializes in things that seem impossible. In fact, He uses ordinary people to do His extraordinary work, and desires to use you! Remove those shackles of inadequacy because you

Create with a purpose.

are witty enough to create new ideas, products, and services. Proverbs 23:7a states, *"For as he thinketh in his heart, so is he."* What do you think about yourself?

My creativity is often spurred by a dissatisfaction with the way things are. Many times, I have insufficient resources to transform my reality, which has required me to improvise and be innovative. As a school teacher, I worked at several summer camps because I needed an additional stream of income. I developed curriculum related to anatomy and physiology, college and career readiness, medicine and the health professions, and science, technology, engineering and mathematics (STEM). While there is nothing wrong with being employed by programs that are already established, I had to fit into their vision and fixed agendas. During one of my summer gigs, I made about $20 per hour teaching middle school students at a local college. While the money was decent and assisted with paying my bills and summer travels, I was disgruntled by the accessibility and affordability of the program. Parents were expected to pay $150 per week for ½ day sessions, or $300 per week for full day with camp only being offered on Monday through Thursday. These prices are typical for quality summer camps, but was not a feasible option for many families, particularly those with multiple children. They offered a few opportunities for scholarships, but overall, the program was not designed to serve the population of students that I was committed to serving. Even if parents received a scholarship, they had to find a way to transport their children during the middle of a work day to a program that was not located in their community. The camp was organized, offered a variety of options for children, and certainly served its purpose for those who could afford it.

I felt as though my gifts and talents were not being utilized to produce the most meaningful results. I traveled 25 minutes across town to teach students who would do well even if I never showed up. There were very few programs being offered in my local community, the majority of which focused on sports and play. Now, it was up to me to create something different. What could I do to prevent the summer learning slide from plaguing students in my own neighborhood - the ones I brushed shoulders with in the grocery store, interacted with at church, or who passed the corridor of my classroom? How could I leverage resources to better serve our community? As a young mother at the time, I longed to create the kind of program that I desired for my son. This journey became personal because I began seeing other people's children as my own. At this very moment, I realized my relentless commitment to something much greater than me - issues of equity and access, and the alleviation of disparities. I have since dedicated my ministry and life to finding solutions to educational and sociological issues by navigating spaces that were not designed for me or people who look like me.

A perfect storm catalyzes a perfect purpose.

It all seemed like a perfect storm. I was dissatisfied with the impact that I was having during the summer months and desired to make more of a difference. I was also transitioning from teaching to becoming a full-time doctoral student and hoped to remain connected with children in my community. Furthermore, my local pastors, Willie and Linda King, desired to see programming being offered for youth during the summer - which could potentially extend into an afterschool program or school. My creativity was going to be exercised further than I could have ever imagined!

I did not have state certifications to officially direct a program, just wild ideas of what opportunities students should be able to access. I would experience the full weight of what it meant to start a program from the ground up and learn how to secure partnerships and garner community support. My pastors called this program FOCUS and valued my expertise and experiences within education to develop a program inclusive of age appropriate curriculum for children. We had a building with 5 classrooms, multipurpose center, computer lab, a full kitchen, and two church vans available to us. I am forever grateful that they gave me an opportunity to create a STEM program to serve children in our community. We had resources at our disposal but needed to secure funding and partnerships to initiate and sustain what we hoped to offer. If this program was going to be successful, I had to launch into the deep and get out of my comfort zone. I attended community meetings, interacted with other faith-based leaders, and leveraged my existing connections as a member of various organizations to provide the initial foundation. The greatest challenge was supporting all facets of the comprehensive program while still making it accessible and affordable to parents. It meant that the church had to assume some of the operational costs such as increased utility and insurance bills. It was time to put our faith to the test and go back to the drawing board. What did I know well? Science. Everything else? Well, I had to learn by experience!

One thing about creating is that there will always be some trial and error involved. You must test, revise, and retest; it's all a part of the engineering design process. I began partnering with local teachers to think through how to create an academic-focused curriculum where participants had opportunities to visit various places in the community. The field trips that I envisioned were atypical for summer programs but could provide students with invaluable experiences. For example, one year, we partnered with Habitat for Humanity for high school participants to build a house in a local neighborhood. We also took students to the autopsy suite in the hospital, the fisheries, and even hiking through a local park. I learned that many of our participants lived within a few miles of the university, but never stepped foot on the campus. I reached out to faculty members to open their laboratories for students to tour and learn about their research. Participants in the program also engaged in project-based learning which often consisted of examining some form of inequity in the community, and how they could collaborate to provide viable solutions. One summer, the middle school students learned about property values and mapped the water filtration facility, recycling transfer station, utility company, waste management, and dump sites on a city map. All these facilities were located on their side of town and so field trips consisted of visiting each place individually to get behind-the-scenes insights into the functionality and technicality involved in operating each one. Participants were charged with asking tough questions about why all these facilities are in their community and the impact it may have on their property values. See Appendix 3 for a sample PBL unit outline.

I had to become creative to ensure that the curriculum would not only be meaningful, but also affordable. Many of the experiential learning field trips did not cost additional funds beyond fuel to run the church vans. Each year I would go through my rolodex to see who I knew, who knew me, and how I could leverage those relationships to provide a unique experience for children in the community. I began to think about who could provide financial support, open their place of employment for a field trip, or facilitate a guest lecture or activity during their day off. Consider the following question - who trusts you enough to know that they will get a good return on investment for supporting your vision? Extraordinary programs are built through long-term and stable partnerships. I understood the importance of strong and healthy relationships and relied on familial support, particularly in the early years, until more substantive partnerships were established. They bought into the vision by donating their time and efforts to keep the books, handle logistics to register the program through the state, provide sponsorships, teach classes, serve as an onsite director, maintain the grounds, and even build the website. It is crucial to build trusting and lasting relationships so that the program becomes one that the community can depend on. We needed to be a face in the community that residents could trust. This meant that we had to find a way to ensure that the program would not be offered one year and gone the next. This is typical of many "good" programs in economically-challenged communities, particularly if initiatives are grant funded; once the grant period ends, so does the program. I was determined not to allow any specific funding mechanism to determine the fate of the program. In launching your youth programs, prioritize securing multiple streams of income - donations, seed money, small grants, parent fees, and even in-kind donations to offset costs.

When God commanded Noah to build an ark, he was building without the presence of rain. His creation did not make much sense because he was operating in faith and obedience. According to Genesis 5:29, Noah's assignment was to comfort

Create even when it does not make sense.

us concerning our work and toil of our hands, due to the land that the Lord had cursed. The book of James teaches us that just as having a body without a spirit is dead, you cannot have faith without works. I had faith that God would bring my dream to pass, but I had to begin acting on it. God spoke to me about how to connect with the body of Christ to grow this program. It was partnerships with local churches and non-profit organizations that helped to sustain it. Not everyone caught the vision immediately, and there were times when people scoffed at me and even tried to derail the program, because they could not see the bigger picture. God showed me a vision of what the program would become and how many families would be blessed by it, but my reality never seemed to align with this vision spurring feelings of discouragement and frustration. I had to realize that it was not for me to "figure out", but rather just walk into what He was doing. My steps were ordered, and everything was going to work out for the good.

Noah's creation was designed to withstand floods and waves. It could hold numerous animals without breaking under pressure. When the waters arose, the ark did not swell, neither did it sink. Resistance forges resilience. It was during the tough times of building, that I realized what it took to launch and grow extraordinary programs. In retrospect, I am grateful for this process because I have the wisdom and experience to mentor others and provide insights that I offer through this guidebook.

When I was a young girl, God revealed to me that I would be able to make a difference in the lives of children. I never dreamed of becoming popular or famous; I just wanted to have influence and bring justice to those who are underserved. Whenever self-doubt would arise, God would send individuals or prophets to confirm the mandate over my life. I was a pre-med student completing difficult science courses, shadowing physicians, and engaging in research on pediatric epilepsy and my own personal research projects related to health disparities. For over a decade, I instructed the Introduction to Health Professions (IHP) course for the

University of Florida College of Medicine's Health Care Summer Institute. I never realized that the knowledge I learned and connections I made along the way would open supernatural doors for children.

During my pre-med journey, I had the privilege of meeting Dr. Albert Robinson III, anesthesiologist and assistant dean for the Office of Diversity and Health Equity. I invited him in as a speaker for the IHP course. After his talk, I asked if he would consider facilitating a Medical Career Outreach Day for 125 students who were enrolled in the summer program I directed at the church. Dr. Robinson asked if he could have a few days to consider this request, and graciously granted it disregarding his hectic and near-impossible work schedule. He connected participants with careers spanning the health professions - physicians, nurses, perfusionists, dentists, pharmacists, and robotic engineers to name a few. Pre-professional (medical and dental) students were also engaged and facilitated breakout sessions. Dr. Robinson was very intentional about recruiting physicians, students, and health professionals of color. Kindergarten through 12th grade participants were introduced to various aspects of medicine through hands-on demonstrations of medical procedures and activities.

Dressed in white lab coats and scrub caps with stethoscopes draped around their necks, students learned how to insert intubations to restore breathing on mannequins. They engaged with robotic engineers as they interacted with virtual patients on a platform where they asked questions to deduce a prognosis. They also did simulations relating to the importance of handwashing to reduce the spread of harmful bacteria, viruses, and diseases. High school students dressed in business attire toting portfolios containing their résumés and participated in mock interviews with professionals that I invited from the community. It all started coming together! My pre-med experience was not about me. Like Noah, I was building without the presence of rain. I was disappointed about receiving interviews but not getting accepted into medical school.

While I was in the process of studying to retake the MCAT so that I could reapply with a stronger application, God interrupted my plans. I spoke with a church minister, Dr. Thomasenia Adams, about needing one more class to be full-time as I was nearing completion of my master's degree. She introduced me to Dr. Rose Pringle and I registered for her Inquiry Based Science course. Although the class met face-to-face on Tuesdays, I was unable to attend most weeks because I was a full-time teacher at the time. So, I capitalized on the fact that I had my own classroom and access to students every day. I made the readings and techniques that she taught me come alive and enacted them immediately in my science instruction. I submitted a portfolio of my reflection with samples of student work for the final assignment and Dr. Pringle scheduled a debriefing session with me in her office. At this meeting, she asked me to discuss my future plans. When I shared that I was studying to retake the MCAT and reapply to medical school, she asked if I had ever considered a PhD in Science Education. Of course, I never even heard of it! It was the furthest thing from my radar. She explained the process and let me know that not only do I belong here, but my work is needed. I prayed about it and everything started to unfold like the ending of a good mystery book. Not only was I accepted into the PhD Program, but I was also awarded the Graduate School Fellowship which provided full tuition and a $25,000 stipend each year. I was getting paid to pursue my education, and it felt so good! God revealed to me that no time was wasted, and everything worked out in His timing and according to His purpose. Dr. Pringle served as my doctoral advisor and wrote the lovely foreword that opened this book.

I was a highly effective educator teaching all levels of biology and chemistry, and God used me as a vessel to expose children to medical careers without having a medical degree. This is one of many examples that I could share about the doors that were opened for children through my life's "failed experiences". I pray that this book will inspire people across this nation and world to be resourceful and create high quality programs within their communities that meet the needs of youth. To whom are you connected? Stop operating in the spirit of rejection and see how the authenticity of your life's experiences can change the lives of children around you.

God saw fit to expose me to high-quality programs as an employee. My job was to be creative and figure out what this kind of program could look like in my particular context, and how I could leverage resources within an economically-challenged community. God did not intend for me to throw away the baby with the bathwater, but instead to understand that He had a plan all along, and my experiences were simply working for a more exceeding and eternal weight of glory. I had something to offer and it was greater than I could have ever imagined!

Don't allow dreamkillers to silence your creativity.

Everyone is not going to understand what you are doing. In fact, at times you may even doubt yourself. But do not give up on what God has promised. The easy road is to accept life the way things are instead of envisioning and working toward something different. You must believe and act on it in faith. Do not allow dreamkillers to tamper with your creativity and detour you from your destiny. When God speaks into your spirit to create, walk in it. You cannot give fear the power to stagnate you, obstruct your sight, or deter you. Be selective about who you give access to your creative space and ideas and persevere even when others do not see your vision. When you're faced with tumultuous situations and scrutiny, keep your eyes fixed on what is unseen. There is a greater purpose behind the work, and God will allow your passions to be fulfilled to achieve your true purpose. Remember that you do not owe carnally-minded individuals a natural explanation for an assignment that is spiritually discerned.

There are many ways to exercise creativity; you do not have to cure cancer or be a rocket scientist. This is a limited and narrow understanding of creativity. You can create your own product, business venture, resource, or program. Distractions occurred, but I

Do not be married to the process; remain focused on the end result.

used them as catalysts to move forward and build greatness. Your purpose is never about you! Too many lives are at stake for you to give up and lose focus of the promise. It takes great strength and courage to block out the noise and continue operating in faith and obedience, particularly when the assignment does not make sense. It takes even greater strength to accept that some people who start with you may not be the same ones who end with you. That, my friends, can be the toughest pill to swallow.

It's easy to expend energies in sticking with the plan instead of remaining fixated on the result. Your plan for launching the program may not align with God's plan, and His route may differ from the one you planned before embarking on this journey. Do not forget to use your spiritual navigation system because it will not lead you astray. God knows how to help you avoid traffic, pitfalls, and danger ahead, if you only trust in Him. When God gives you a vision, He often does not reveal "the how". This is only experienced through the process.

The location of the inaugural STEM program was strategically selected to meet the specific needs of the community. According to zipatlas.com (2018), the zip code where the program was initiated has troubling statistics related to educational and income disparities – 30% of the population over 25 years old do not hold a high school diploma or its equivalent compared to the national average of 19.6%. Most residents have unskilled service-oriented jobs with 22% of the households earning less than $10,000 each year which is more than double the state and national average of about 10%. Furthermore, the property value for 45% of the homes is less than $50,000 (national average is 10%) with 93% of homes valuing less than $100,000 (national average is 41%). Situated in this community, the program seeks to provide access to STEM for social justice and hopes that exposure will break the cycle of intergenerational poverty. This commitment to social justice toward the empowerment of underserved groups to eliminate poverty is the result and driving force behind my life's assignment and Kingdom purpose.

The world does not end at your corner store!

Parents and students shared testimonials about being tested for the gifted program or accepted into magnet/accelerated programs. Students saw options and realized that there was more to their neighborhood than the local corner store. These stores are typically referred to as convenience stores for a reason. They provide the essentials so that you do not have to travel any further to get what you need. Corner stores are typically connected to a gas station and owned by someone who does not live in that community. In operating STEM programs, I have learned that representation and exposure are essential! Sometimes you must travel outside of your neighborhood to see a Black physician, attorney, or engineer. When designing curriculum, representation should not be an afterthought! Students need to be exposed to much more than disciplinary content. There is so much more to see, do, and experience. They need to be taught how to approach every situation with skepticism and not take everything at face value. We must encourage our children to be change agents in their communities. Graduation and poverty rates will change once mindsets do! Our children no longer must become products of their environment; they have the power to actively change it. They can start envisioning themselves as entrepreneurs, owning properties and businesses that will bring wealth into their communities, and leave behind an inheritance for generations to come.

Nadja Holland, I AM STEM Participant and Intern

I have had the privilege of participating in I AM STEM for the past few summers. I had the opportunity to be an intern for the summer camp which allowed me to receive numerous volunteer hours. One of Florida's graduation requirements is to have at least 100 volunteer hours, but with I AM STEM, I was able to triple that in one summer. As an intern, I was assigned to the 4-year old classroom where I collaborated with a teacher to facilitate math, science, and engineering projects. As I was teaching the younger children, I learned a lot during the process. I had to be patient with the children and do things right the first time around. I also had an opportunity to attend multiple college tours and engage in other summer institutes. I must say that these trips were extremely beneficial because I am graduating from Eastside High School this year and leaving for college. This camp has exposed me to many opportunities and has prepared me to be successful in school. Interning with I AM STEM has had a huge impact on me. I now realize the importance of giving back, because it gives hope. I AM STEM gave me hope. Where there is hope, there is always a future!

Nature operates under God's command.

We must understand that God created us and is mindful of us. We cannot fulfill our life's purpose in our own strength, or there would be no need for Him. We need divine intervention and for God to equip us with the necessary tools, resources, and connections to carry out His work. God is polishing our gifts, so that we can create and teach others by our example. When you take creativity and infuse it with godly obedience, you will produce in the earthly realm what God has revealed to you through His spirit.

Revelation 4:11- *Thou art worthy, O Lord, to receive glory and honour and power: for thou hast created all things, and for thy pleasure they are and were created.*

God remains the same, but the days are becoming more evil. The Church does not need to lose its footing. Our next scientists need to know who Jesus is and design creations that will not only bring God glory but will be of earthly benefit. The next executives and entrepreneurs, influencers, decision-makers, and those in authority need to have a personal relationship with Jesus Christ. So, what are we doing as a church to create spaces that nurture this kind of creativity? How is the church engaging with youth beyond addressing spiritual and charitable needs? Are our spaces being used to truly build the body of Christ? Who is benefiting from the church's presence in the community? Is that presence being felt or are we becoming reduced to mere brick and mortar?

Contemplative Questions:

1) What is hindering you from exercising your creativity?

_____

_____

_____

_____

2) How do you envision your role in the community?

_____

_____

_____

_____

3) What programs or services do you currently offer?

_____

_____

_____

_____

4) What age groups or needs are still unmet?

_____

_____

_____

5) Do you have the capacity to meet those needs?

_____

_____

_____

_____

6) What has God instructed you to do? Have you moved on it yet?

   _____

   _____

   _____

   _____

7) List innovative ways that you can become more engaged in youth programming (as an individual and church family).

   _____

   _____

   _____

   _____

PRACTICE 2
LOVE THY NEIGHBOR AS THYSELF

Hebrews 6:10 - For God is not unrighteous to forget your work and labour of love, which ye have shewed toward his name, in that ye have ministered to the saints, and do minister.

God has given us the power to exercise creativity, but it all starts with an important seed - LOVE! Love should be at the center of everything that we do because to truly reach people, they must first know that we care. When we help God's people, He is not unjust to forget our work and labor of love. The late Dr. Martin Luther King Jr. said "Power without love is reckless and abusive, and love without power is sentimental and anemic. Power at its best is love implementing the demands of justice, and justice at its best is power correcting everything that stands against love." It's not enough to be an influencer. How are you using that influence? Have you incorporated the love of Christ into your work? How are you manifesting God's love toward others?

I John 4:7-9
7- Beloved, let us love one another: for love is of God; and everyone that loveth is born of God, and knoweth God.
8 - He that loveth not knoweth not God; for God is love.

9- In this was manifested the love of God toward us,
because that God sent his only begotten Son into the world,
that we might live through him.

It is easy to love people who share similar values and beliefs, but much more difficult to extend that same courtesy to those who have refused, abused, or misused your love. In developing youth programs, we must remember to love individuals who are hurt, and those who may not know how to love in return.

When you lead with the love of Christ, no one is "unloveable". In fact, those who hurt the most are the ones we are required to love the most. We were never commanded to judge or determine who is worthy of love and acceptance. Simply put, this is not the job of the saints. God is the ultimate vindicator who will judge us according to our deeds. We must teach the word and allow God to bring conviction and condemnation.

Matthew 7:1 - Judge not, that ye be not judged.

Currently, people are so focused on self-gain, elevation, and social media likes that they have forsaken God's command to love others. We measure our self-worth based on the approval of individuals who are not connected to our purpose, and have a difficult time truly loving our perfectly imperfect selves. What becomes even more challenging is figuring out a way to love others, when we are still learning how to love ourselves. Life has taught me that your *teaching* will only take you as far as your *being*. If you are not practicing what you preach, people are less apt to receive your instruction. It is essential to exude Christ's love and mannerisms in all that we do. Our daily interactions should literally reflect the love of Jesus Christ. When I was younger, I remember people wearing the WWJD bracelets to remind themselves about what Jesus would do in certain situations. We cannot behave as our flesh would suppose, but the Holy Spirit should lead our actions.

Matthew 22:37-40

37 - Jesus said unto him, Thou shalt love the Lord thy God with all thy heart, and with all thy soul, and with all thy mind.
38 - This is the first and great commandment.
39 - And the second is like unto it, Thou shalt love thy neighbor as thyself.
40 - On these two commandments hang all the law and the prophets.

Throughout my young adult life, Mommy used to quote a famous saying by William J. Toms warning us to be careful of the life we lead, because we may be the only Bible that some people read. I have taken this to heart! I rarely get behind a pulpit to preach the word because I am not an ordained pastor, just a willing vessel who loves the Lord and His people. I make every effort to exemplify the Love of Christ through my words and deeds and work tirelessly to ensure alignment between the two. In our pursuit to develop extraordinary youth programs, we must remember the spiritual aspect of whole child development. We interact with hurting children and families who may long for a hug or someone to simply say, "I love you". You don't know the trauma that some children have endured, and your STEM curriculum will be meaningless without having mechanisms in place to address it. We cannot get caught up in the intricacies of program development that we forget to water the roots. Every program must be rooted and grounded in love! One of the I AM STEM sites starts each day with family meetings and affirmations while another begins with prayer and recitation of scriptures. This is intentionally done to validate students' existence and their multidimensional identities. You can adjust what you do based on the population of students being served, but there must be opportunities for children to be reminded of their giftedness, intelligence, and belongingness.

You have to love me before you can "save" me.

John 3:16 - For God so LOVED the world that He gave His only begotten son that whosoever believeth on Him should not perish but have everlasting life.

Love is a 4-letter word that is simple, yet so complicated. It requires us to dive into ourselves and meet people where they are without having preconceived intentions of changing them. Believe me, people will change once they experience the true love of Jesus Christ. It's all in His timing! God loved us that He gave His only son- this biblical principle is one that is still relevant today. Jesus was the sacrifice for our sins, and salvation was made possible because of this great act of love. We must learn how to love <u>and</u> give in order to reach a hurting community. As Christians, we try to win souls for Christ, but grab our binoculars to zoom in on one's faults, shortcomings, mishaps, and mistakes. The reality is that individuals who are the most critical of others, are typically the ones who have the most to hide. The Bible reminds us that love covers a multitude of sins. We are imperfect people serving imperfect people! All too often, there are contingencies on our love - strings attached, red tape, and unreasonable conditions. This often makes individuals refrain from coming to the House of God for fear of being ridiculed and condemned. God is the greatest lover; His love is unearned, unmerited, and undeserved. As His children, we ought to model His example of pure love. Love that is patient, kind, and free of hidden agendas. According to Galatians 5:22, the first fruit of the Spirit is… you guessed it, LOVE!

Hebrews 13:1-2
1 – Let brotherly love continue
2 – Be not forgetful to entertain strangers for you have entertained angels unaware.

The church is divided by the size of the congregation, denomination, and location. It leads me to ask the following question – Are we the real hindrance? Children have an easier time looking past social factors that create division than adults. What are we

To create extraordinary youth programs, we must first deal with the psyche of adults.

doing to forge healthy and loving relationships within our churches, across ministries, and in the community? Many churches typically offer Sunday School or Children's Church during the regularly scheduled services and occasionally offer a short Vacation Bible School during the summer. We need to broaden the types of programs that we implement to attract and serve more children and families.

As Christians, we tend to box God in and limit His abilities based on our personal experiences and current reality. As a science educator, I have the privilege of training pre-service teachers, and constantly remind them to resist the urge to teach how they were taught. Lectures may have worked for them, but the curriculum, standards, and state assessments are requiring students to synthesize information and not just regurgitate it. You will not get different results by using the same old approaches. There is a time and place for lecturing, but you must be willing to try innovative and student-driven methods. News alert! Students are not going home to talk about your lecture. Students must experience the science, not just read about it from outdated textbooks or listen to you talk about it. They may go home and discuss an experiment, demonstration, or even a nature walk, and so we need to embed these types of opportunities in our programs. For example, you can allow students to engage in argumentation to determine whether the world is circular or flat. They will be expected to conduct their own research to differentiate between real news and fake news. Times have changed. Policies change, standards change, initiatives change, and most of all, children change! So, adults must be willing to change their approaches and thinking to be more effective in reaching and teaching children.

How are we showing the love of God to people who don't look like us or may not even smell like us? What outreach events are we doing to meet the real needs of the community? Furthermore, what services are we offering to help children develop 21st century skills such as creativity, critical thinking, collaboration, and communication?

The hardest part about starting is turning the key in the ignition!

Faith-based leaders and Christians are seeking ways to engage with the community, but do not know where to begin. The first step is to get off the church campus! Once you're in the community, the next step is to listen. This is not the time to make assumptions. To effectively respond to the needs, you must stop talking long enough to hear what they are. The church is here to serve, not to be served. So, receive whatever is said (and unsaid) in the spirit of love, because love conquers all. There will be individuals who reject you, but that should not change your approach. Stick with the game plan! It's not for vain glory or pleasure.

Love should permeate throughout all aspects of our youth programs from the way that we greet students in the morning to how we interact with their parents. Love until it hurts and then find it in you to love harder and give a little deeper. Don't leave this earth with gifts and purpose trapped inside of you. Gain the strength that you need to launch and grow programs that will bless your community.

__Hebrews 5:12__ – For when for the time ye ought to be teachers, ye have need that one teach you again which be the first principles of the oracles of God: and are become such as have need of milk and not of strong meat.

You've got too much purpose to be petty!

To experience the love of Christ and share that love with others, you've got to be willing to choose your battles. Everything does not require your attention! So, don't sweat the small stuff or tire yourself with things that are irrelevant. Get back to the basics and live on purpose for purpose. Let's expend a lot less energy focusing on the outward appearance and spend more time dealing with issues of the heart. We need to master the elementary truths of God's word so that we can teach others.

There were many times when I could have focused on minute things and forfeit my purpose. I remember being agitated because we were offering a program that children needed but could not get parents to make that commitment or investment to enroll their children. I would hear parents complain about their children's low performance in school and how they failed standardized tests and witnessed them sacrificing to pay for a pair of name brand sneakers instead of academic enrichment or tutoring. Here I was working tirelessly to remove almost every barrier to give them access to the appropriate resources and services and being caught up in my feelings because they did not respond immediately. I cried real tears trying to figure out how to birth the types of programs that I felt our children deserved. God had to deal with me and reveal that it was not my responsibility to show people my worth or the value of the program; my assignment was simply to continue building and carrying out His purpose.

Year after year, the program grew and became a blessing to families outside of the community. Parents were literally driving to our side of town to enroll their children in this high-quality program that was a fraction of the cost of what they were paying elsewhere. Once parents in our community saw others taking advantage of this opportunity, they joined the bandwagon. I did not have to host Come-to-Jesus sessions to convince them anymore. Word of mouth traveled quickly and efficiently! Parents felt like their children were missing out, and we got to reap the intended results. Remember to stay focused on the assignment. Pettiness is simply a distraction to your purpose; your response to setbacks must be different!

Do not focus on things that have no bearing on your destiny. They are called distractions! I could have focused on who talked about me, tried to sabotage my destiny or frustrate my purpose. My energies would have been misplaced which could have caused me to miss what God was trying to do in that season. God graced me with spiritual guidance and I owe it to the world to share it through the pages of this book. There are people who need to hear my story because their assignment is connected to my obedience. Through this obedience came repositioning where God literally reserved seats at different tables to make an even greater impact on a national and global level.

Know your why!

Know your Why BEFORE beginning your program. If your "why" is not grounded in love and serving the community, it is shallow and not worth pursuing! This work is difficult and can be strenuous particularly on the host site. You will need to make sure logistics are adequately addressed – facilities meet the state requirements and pass inspections, proper insurance coverage is in place, financial accounts are set up, safety and evacuation plans are created, restrooms are working, the A/C Heating System is functioning properly, supplies are purchased, meals and snacks are scheduled with allergies being accounted for, all staff have received a Level II Background screening, and a portion of the staff is CPR and First Aid certified. There are so many considerations!

If you want a pleasant experience, you have to create it. Having procedures in place and the right staff who can effectively teach children and interact well with others is essential. Stressors will come; that's a promise! You may have to overlook the foolishness and focus on the favor that God gave you to operate despite it. Believe me, it will take some time to figure things out, but once you know your why, pettiness won't have a place in carrying out God's plan for your life.

In learning how to love our neighbors as ourselves, we must remember the importance of open communication, and finding ways to collaborate rather than compete. It may be a good idea to survey the  **Collaboration over competition.** community and see what resources and services are already being offered and what needs still have not yet been met. See if you have the means to be a solution to the problem and ability to work within that community. If there are 100 different STEM camps being offered in your community, you do not need to start another one. Maybe you can just collaborate and strengthen an already existing program, unless there is a clear gap that you are filling. Your church can provide sponsorships for children in a local neighborhood to attend. For me, there were programs being offered, but they were not affordable or accessible to the students that needed them the most. Furthermore, they were narrowly focused and did not consider the many other factors that determine if children of color will respond to the curriculum. The curriculum did not attend to their cultural resources or provide opportunities for parents to be involved in meaningful ways. Therefore, I had to be innovative in how to meet a need that could potentially change the trajectory of the whole community. As a ministry, collaborate to uncover the strengths of your congregation. If you have entrepreneurs and business owners in your membership, you could possibly offer an entrepreneurship and leadership program. Leverage the gifts and talents of those who are involved to determine a focal area that can address a community need.

Remember, you do not need to reinvent the wheel. If you have the right organizations and partnerships in place, you can increase your capacity to sustain programming because more individuals are vested. Furthermore, many hands make light work and so you're no longer expected to be an expert at everything! Rather, you create comprehensive and high-quality programs by leveraging the expertise of the individuals, organizations, and partnerships involved. For example, one of my friends, Ross Ridgewell, worked for

IBM. They have community engagement initiatives where they apply their talents and technology to solve societal issues. We offered financial literacy on Fridays and called it Financial Fridays. Ross garnered support of his colleagues to serve and complete their Summit volunteering. Through a series of conference calls and email exchanges, we created grade-appropriate lesson plans and interactive modules that they implemented. The curriculum ranged from teaching children the value of money and how to calculate change, to learning about the stock market, investing, budgeting, credit cards, and financing college. As part of the STEM curriculum, we offered financial literacy classes and had a voice in the curriculum but did not need to provide the human capital or expertise to ensure its success.

Confirm that you have access to the necessary skill sets to implement what you market, and that the service is needed. Do not overpromise and underdeliver! I no longer have to "sell" the program because I provided a viable solution to a need, and now the community is actively working to sustain it. When you have created something inspired by God, there is no need to compete. I gave God my best and sowed the gifts that He bestowed upon me. It is in His nature to perform multiplicative blessings. All I have to do is be obedient and do His work with love.

When you operate in the spirit of love, it will transcend to the children and families connected to the program and become evident in the projects they produce. One prime example is from an assignment where high school scholars participating I AM STEM Camp were tasked to use technology to create public service announcements and informational videos. Gabrielle Welch made a stop motion video by writing a poem to her fellow peers entitled "Dear Black Kings and Queens".

Dear Black Kings and Queens,
In this world,
People are looking for you to fail.
So much that people are building cells in jail
Just because of your existence.
Instead of people judging you for what's inside,
They judge you for the race you identify with.
But you must remember to be the best that you can be.
Sometimes you may not see how important you are,
But you are a star, in a world full of dirt.
You're gonna cry, you're gonna hurt,
But don't let that stop you from knowing your worth.
Dear my Black Kings and Queens,
Remember you're amazing and follow your dreams!

Love begets love! Let's transform our psyche and be great examples to our youth to give the next generation a promising future.

Contemplative Questions:

1) How is your love being manifested in the community?

_____

_____

_____

_____

2) What is your "why" for engaging in youth development programs?

_____

_____

_____

_____

3) What aspects of your thinking may need to be transformed for more effective engagement with youth?

_____

_____

_____

_____

4) How can you foster more collaboration in your community?

_____

_____

_____

_____

PRACTICE 3
WE ARE LABORERS TOGETHER
WITH GOD

Psalm 133:1 – Behold, how good and pleasant it is for
brethren to dwell together in unity!

This practice is a logical continuation of Practice #2 that centered on brotherly love. Discord and confusion make it difficult to run extraordinary programs. The Holy Bible encourages us to live together in peace, and so I want to emphasize the importance of strong leadership, transparency, and unity.

Romans 12:18 – If it be possible, as much as lieth in you,
live peaceably with all men.

I Corinthians 14:33 – For God is not the author of
confusion, but of peace, as in all churches of the saints.

Unity does not occur by happenstance. You must intentionally create and maintain a unified stance! In discussing unity, we cannot ignore leadership. Be selective about who you place into leadership positions because it impacts the whole program. Are your leaders welcoming and compassionate, or mean and abrasive? Do they know how to interact with parents? Are they organized? Can you trust them to collect and deposit payments and have access

Leadership is too important to be an afterthought.

to bank accounts? Do they have computer and writing skills to craft letters and notices? Do they understand the target population being served? What skillsets and experiences do they bring to the table? Do they fit into the overall vision and mission of the organization? Do they position themselves as learners? What are their motives for leading and are they pure?

When I assumed a faculty position at Georgia State University, it required me to relocate to another state. I was determined to train someone who would be committed to continuing the work in Florida. In my search for an onsite director, I specifically prayed for God to send an individual who had my heart. In a roundabout, God kind of way, He placed Nasseeka Denis in my path. She did not have a background in education, and her mannerisms were quite different from mine in that she was extremely quiet and introverted. I felt apprehensive and a little anxious about the transition. However, I rest assured in knowing that she was just as passionate about working with children in the community. As an educator, I am trained to teach content and skills. To me, that is the easy part. Nasseeka leads with integrity and has a spirit to serve God's people; these character traits are not easily taught and are developed over a lifetime. Through her experiences serving as an onsite director, Nasseeka has developed strong interpersonal skills and is more knowledgeable about curriculum development and how to run the business aspect of the program. She continues to oversee an I AM STEM Camp site in Gainesville, FL and now serves as the onsite director of an afterschool program as well.

Ms. Nasseeka Denis, I AM STEM Onsite Director at Caring and Sharing Learning School

In 2016, I was finishing up my undergraduate studies. At that time, I made the decision to change career paths to youth development, but I did not know where to begin. I always think back on how I met Dr. King, a blessing and an answer to my prayers to work in the community. She mentored me and gave me an opportunity to serve as the onsite director. I was very timid and even more soft spoken than I am now. Despite having those qualities that can be seen as setbacks, she gave me a chance and pushed me so that I had no choice but to speak up and become a leader.

Now that I am preparing for my fourth summer as an onsite director, I am thankful for the lessons that I learned, and growth that has taken place over time. I am now more confident leading a team of teachers and staff, communicating with parents, and interacting with our young scholars. I have had the opportunity to learn from and work with amazing community partners who constantly share their wisdom to help me improve as a young professional. Every summer, I am ready to interact with our youth activists who are becoming movers and shakers in our community.

I have personally seen this program impact over 400 students and their families. Students attend camp with a sense of urgency and excitement to explore the different STEM disciplines. Our parents believe in the program wholeheartedly and recruit their friends, family, and even strangers! They understand the value of children of color finding an identity in STEM. Our community, one that lacks representation in STEM, now consists of youth who are passionate about exploring different STEM careers.

I am thankful for Dr. King on both a personal and professional level. To be led by someone who has a heart for the community and our youth is so amazing. She pushes me to further myself as an individual educationally and in my career. I always look forward to camp and seeing the students' excitement about learning.

In leadership, two important areas need to be addressed – accountability and support! The onsite director should be held accountable to certain standards and report to executive directors or a board of directors. More importantly, onsite directors need to be well-supported as they stand on the front line to develop and implement programs. It is crucial to have individuals in place to handle financials, assist with

Extraordinary programs must be kingdom driven not personality driven.

website development, recruitment, purchasing supplies, and securing sponsorships and partnerships. There are many areas that deserve consideration when running youth programs, and the onus cannot be left on the onsite director alone. Working collaboratively will prevent burnout so that your director does not operate under stress and project that stress onto the teaching staff or families being served.

Strong leadership is essential and should not be based on convenience. Spend time searching for the right person to assume this role. Not everyone who wants the position possesses the necessary expertise and character traits, which can in turn jeopardize the quality of the program. Remember that if the head is sick, the whole program will be impacted. You need someone who will operate with a spirit of excellence and lead by example. Not a leader who relies on micromanaging and is unwilling to make the same sacrifices that they require of others.

Be selective about who you place into leadership, and then recruit and train qualified individuals who are the right fit and understand the vision. As a leader, you may not physically be on campus every day, but the program should still run smoothly even without your presence. Ensure that your programs are kingdom driven and not personality driven because life happens. People get sick, relocate, and even pass away. The only way your program will survive major changes is if a strong infrastructure is in place.

Be intentional about being on one accord.

To promote unity, you may have to meet frequently (especially if you are just launching youth programs), so that everyone is on the same page. You cannot merely tolerate each other, but truly commune together for a shared purpose. Unity is rare and pleasant, but God will command a blessing where there is oneness of faith and oneness of thought. If you do not have a vision and mission statement, come together to write one so that everyone is working toward a common goal. Continue to meet regularly to maintain open lines of communication. These meetings should not just be an agenda item on your standard leadership meetings, but standalone meetings that focus specifically on how to develop, implement, and support programs that meet the needs of families in your community.

In the beginning of this book, I included a short section that focused on getting readers on the same page. This may be one of the most important parts of the book because it offers clarity about the lens that I used to inform my writing. It's based on my own lived experiences in the church and working for and directing STEM programs for the past decade. I have no idea who will read this book, but their lived experiences and even motives for engaging in youth development may differ from mine. I have no control over that but can be transparent about my purpose for writing the book and meaning behind the title. In academia, we discuss the importance of ontology and epistemology. Ontology refers to the study of being and beliefs about truth and reality. People typically subscribe to realism or relativism where they either believe that there is an objective Truth or that truth is contextual and based on the situation or context. We also talk about epistemology, or the study of knowledge, where researchers share their relationship to the study based on their worldviews. Ontology and epistemology often set the foundation and determine how scholars approach their work. They influence every decision being made from selection of frameworks, methodology, and methods employed, to how the results are analyzed and presented. So, what does ontology and epistemology have to do with youth programs? Your clarity and transparency about your purpose and worldview will promote unity and minimize confusion.

Seek transparency over illusions.

The beauty of magic shows is that they function off illusions. There is so much that happens behind the scene than meets the natural eye. People show their appreciation of spectacular shows with gasps and applause, but it's designed that they never know what's taking place behind the curtains or fancy hand gestures. When you're developing community-based programs, it is important to seek transparency rather than illusions. You don't want people being awed by a program but disengaged in the work to make it happen. Their awe should come from seeing how everything unfolds with entities working together, exciting curriculum, and children's lives being changed. Your stakeholders are a part of the story and need to work behind-the-scenes to make high quality programs unfold for the community.

Recently, I spoke at a Career Day and entitled my presentation "When Life Tells You No". During my talk, I revealed my failures and the many rejections that I endured during my journey. I thought that I was losing, but God was building patience, putting the right people in place, and orchestrating my steps for His great work. It was not until I had enough courage to tell my story that it all started making sense. People gloat over your successes but cannot readily relate because their lives are not as picturesque as the illusion of yours. When we error on the side of transparency, we no longer feel the need to cover up painful parts of the process because we realize that everything is all a part of a greater story that will work together for our good.

In 2012, when we first started a STEM camp at the church, it was a 5-week program that lasted from 8am-2pm. After the program ended, I facilitated focus group interviews and asked stakeholders how the program could be improved to better serve the needs of their families. Parents discussed transportation being an issue and the difficulty they experienced in arranging for their children to be picked up during the middle of a work day. From there, we redesigned the program and included an afterhours component where parents had an option to pay the same rate and pick up their children at 2pm or pay a little extra for an extended day which ended at 5:30pm. Well, many parents did not sign up for afterhours care but ended up leaving their children way past the 2pm time. From there, we developed a full-day, 10-hour program (7:30am-5:30pm) where parents had the flexibility to pick up their children early, but it was designed to ensure that proper personnel and teacher-student ratios were met throughout the course of the full day. We did not paint an illusion that we got it right the first time, but as we negotiated the needs of parents and ability/availability of the staff and teachers, we met in a place where everyone was satisfied and included in the decision-making process.

Illusions are only good until the trick is exposed; thus, magicians never reveal their secrets to knowingly deceive the audience. Do not allow issues to sit and fester while expending energy masking and concealing what you can fix. Dysfunction, when unaddressed, begets more dysfunction, which can manifest itself in various forms that are unhealthy for (and potentially destructive to) the program and families being served. The disappearing and reappearing act is not conducive for this type or work. You will find that that the greatest compliment of a program is valuing transparency and inclusivity. Let's work toward this end to ensure that all things are done with the spirit of excellence and in the best interests of all stakeholders.

I Corinthians 1:10 – *Now I beseech you brethren, by the name of our Lord Jesus Christ, that ye all speak the same thing, and that there be no divisions among you; but that ye be perfectly joined together in the same mind and in the same judgement.*

Create spaces that involve a variety of voices, experiences, and expertise. Rethink how authority is distributed so that the decision-making process is not top-down, but inclusive of many stakeholders. Administer evaluation surveys and focus groups for parents, teachers, and students to get feedback on what went well and how the program can be improved to better serve their needs.

Program decisions and revisions should be based on feedback from your own parents, and not just on what other programs are doing. It is good to get ideas off the internet, but not in lieu of listening to the concerns of those who are vested in your program.

Encourage and foster intergenerational relationships.

Intergenerational relationships are a staple for extraordinary youth programs because you have individuals from all walks of life coming together for a shared goal of bettering their communities by investing in children and their families. These relationships should mirror the larger cultural environment and include youth, near peer mentors, young adults, middle aged adults, and seasoned seniors who carry a wealth of historical knowledge. All age groups provide different strengths and knowledge. Therefore, a certain level of respect <u>must</u> be maintained in their interactions amongst each other to reap the full benefits of these relationships. The more intently you listen (for understanding and not just to offer a response), the more you can learn, and lead with intentionality and purpose. Today when the country is so divided, let's set an example of unity by forsaking individualistic agendas to collectively focus on larger societal and humanitarian concerns.

In thinking about intergenerational relationships, the famous African proverb comes to mind that "it takes a village to raise a child". I have developed and implemented an interdisciplinary seminar at Georgia State University (GSU) titled, *It Takes A Village to Train A Scientist.* This course introduced undergraduate scholars to programs and organizations at GSU and the greater Atlanta constituency that are committed to youth education in formal and informal settings. In conceptualizing course objectives, activities, and outcomes, I wanted to push the boundaries on the types of experiences that students were afforded as they pursued their college degrees. I desired to design a course where students took ownership of their learning while promoting access and equity in STEM education and developing soft skills to

It takes a village to train a scientist.

become socially responsible and engaged citizens. Most of all, I hoped to find a way for students to earn course credit by working to break down barriers that exist between institutions of higher education (IHEs), community-based organizations, businesses, and K-12 schools. Undergraduates networked within their communities and developed action plans for how different entities can collaborate to provide comprehensive experiences for K-12 students. They also explored how various stakeholders could work with parents to effectively prepare their children to become productive and informed citizens in society. This experiential learning seminar engaged GSU undergraduates in field trips, guest speaker presentations, scholarly readings, reflections, and service learning projects to develop authentic community-based partnerships to effectively prepare this generation of scientists and scientifically literate citizens.

My first year implementing the course, we partnered with Coretta Scott King Young Women's Leadership Academy (CSKYWLA) in Atlanta, GA. The undergraduates selected this school because the district sought to close its doors in 2017, but parents and community members fought to keep the school open. They were excited about the positive impact this collaboration could have on the students, particularly because CSKYWLA was in the process of seeking STEM certification (and the entire class consisted of STEM majors). CSKYWLA is the only all-girls, public, single gender school in the Atlanta Public Schools system. It serves approximately 400 6th-12th grade students, 100% of whom are Black and Latina. CSKYWLA is the school's acronym and has been given the following definition – "to be empowered by scholarship, non-violence, and social change, my sister". CSKYWLA predominantly serves economically challenged students and 100% of their student population receives free breakfast and lunch through the Community Eligibility Provisions Nutrition Program. The school's attendance zone draws primarily from a zip code with some of the highest crime and poverty rates in the city of Atlanta. Despite the economic disadvantages that their students face, the administrators and teachers strive to (1) provide a rigorous college preparatory curriculum to ensure that CSKYWLA ladies are college and career ready, (2) develop the next generation of women in STEM, (3) embrace diversity and inclusiveness as an essential component in the ways they educate the girls, and (4) contribute positively to their community and environment on a global scale.

Some of the major highlights of the course were that GSU Undergraduates facilitated a garden reboot day to revitalize the community edible garden at CSKYWLA. This school is in a food desert and so they solicited and received donations for plants, soil, seeds, and compost and spent an afternoon with middle school students turning the soil and planting herbs and vegetables. They also facilitated a toiletry drive to collect hygiene items for the Parent Resource Center and partnered with a local church to receive a $500 donation to sponsor the Chief Science Officers Program to give students a voice in STEM education within their schools and community.

Furthermore, GSU students secured 5 full-paid scholarships for middle and high school girls to visit the Cornell Lab of Ornithology and engage with researchers and develop their own conservation projects. One of the GSU students who worked on this project during the semester course served as a chaperone for the trip alongside a CSKYWLA science teacher. For the culminating event, undergraduates hosted a Community Forum for the school where they brought in representatives from local non-profit organizations, industry partners, and institutions of higher education to share about available STEM opportunities.

Why did I take the time to share all of this? Because there is power in collaboration and partnerships. Scholars and practitioners are discussing the importance of creating communities of practice in the form of STEM Learning Ecosystems. These ecosystems provide cross-sector learning and make STEM-rich environments accessible to all children. They foster dynamic collaborations among entities to improve STEM literacy, diversity, equity, and inclusion. The more you work across entities, the more you realize how everything is interconnected. We are attacking similar issues, utilizing different approaches...in silos! We need to know our limitations and what we can be accomplished in our own strength. How much more can we accomplish with the assistance of others? Remember, you cannot do it all, and you should not do it alone! Do not be afraid to think outside of the box and cross institutional lines. Partner with others who have the expertise or resources that you need to get your intended results. Strong partnerships are your greatest resource and are initiated and sustained through relationship-building. Remember, churches are a vital part of your village and are well-positioned to enact change and in the community. Don't be afraid to use STEM Education as a mechanism to establish community because true transformation will occur through unified partnerships.

Wendy Roche, Local Missions Coordinator, Greenhouse Church, Gainesville, FL

For the past five years, as a church, Greenhouse has had the opportunity to partner with FOCUS and I AM STEM. As someone whose work is central to the East Gainesville community, it does not take long to realize where many resources are lacking. A major part of Greenhouse's heart is to step outside of the church walls and get our congregation involved and aware of the issues or needs that are in our community. We also recognize that we do not have the ability to meet every single need or to do it well unless we partner with other organizations and individuals who are doing so successfully.

My specific role as Local Missions Coordinator includes helping bridge the gap with the reality of what is taking place in our communities and how to address those realities - oftentimes presented as injustices and broken systems. I see firsthand and hear stories from the families and children I have the privilege of working with, the lack of opportunities they face or the inability to meet certain opportunities. One such example is not having many summer programs available in East Gainesville. Families I interact with have told me that there are programs on the other side of town they have been interested in but are either out of their geographic area or they do not have the financial capacity. We are aware that due to the lack of opportunities, children can easily find themselves in negative situations. Almost every parent I know wants his or her child to be involved in something constructive during the summer time. Once we realized how necessary this was and knowing that none of the programs we offered as a church fully operated in the summer, we knew we had to partner with I AM STEM. I still remember the first few children from the families we personally served who participated. Their mindsets changed due to the exposure of different activities at camp. They had fun learning educational material and overall felt like they had a productive summer. Their parents were so grateful to see the change in their children, particularly because their summer was not wasted.

To me, I AM STEM is the epitome of the kind of programs we need in areas such as East Gainesville. It allows students to reach their potential by being around positive and successful individuals from different career fields who they can relate to. Many students in East Gainesville are limited when it comes to knowing and being interested in the STEM fields. I believe representation is key to changing this, not only with how STEM fields are presented, but also who is doing the presenting. The fact that I AM STEM takes this approach in a holistic manner where you can see the change and growth in these students year after year, has made it easy to continue supporting the program.

Dr. King, thank you for giving our children the ability to dream, to recognize their potential in different fields especially those relating to STEM. Thank you for preparing them to be agents of change in our community by allowing them to see what the world has to offer and that they have what it takes to enact change. Thank you for providing our youth with everyday life skills that will allow them to be responsible and productive citizens in society. We are grateful for your efforts to close the many gaps in our

*community because of what you provide through your
programs. Thank you again and again!*

Contemplative Questions:

1) What attention have you given to establishing effective leadership for your programs? What are you doing well and what adjustments can be made?

_____

_____

_____

_____

_____

2) In your quest to becoming more transparent, what are some tangible things that you can do to embrace transparency over illusions?

_____

_____

_____

_____

_____

3) What is the mission and vision of your educational and youth programs? If you do not currently have any, begin thinking about what they might be.

_____

_____

_____

_____

_____

4) List some of your personal and organizational strengths. What are areas of growth?

_____

_____

_____

_____

_____

5) Brainstorm how you can collaborate with different entities to strengthen your areas of growth and develop an ecosystem.

_____

_____

_____

_____

_____

PRACTICE 4
LET YOUR LIGHT SO SHINE
BEFORE MEN

The Light

Verse 1

When you're feeling like just giving up
Life's just too hard at times
You have your family to take care of
And all you're left with is just dimes
I have a God who sees your suffering
And you crying there at night
He said that's just your test and trial
Through all your darkness there's a light

Chorus

The light that gives me strength
Keeps me from all harm
The light that tells me to just hold on
The light that when I am tested,
It gives me joy, peace, and happiness
The light, the light of God

Verse 2

When your family and friends forsake you
And there's no one to turn to

You tried all these worldly pleasures, the devil offered you
Though the road may seem just rough right now,
There will be a brighter day,
The Lord sees His child unhappy,
And through the billows makes a way

Bridge
Nobody knows what I've been through,
But they see me now as a vessel that God flows through
He will do the same for you
Give you that light that tells you to just hold on, Be strong

This chapter is very special to me because this principle is personal and requires internal transformation through reflection and introspection. Growing up in a family of seven was exciting, and never had a dull moment! We laughed hard, played hard, and sometimes even fought hard! Another reality was that we rarely had much privacy or quiet time. Many days I would steal away to the bathroom, make myself comfortable on the toilet, and journal. Even though we lived in a two-parent household, we struggled! It seemed like our friends lived in nice houses and wore trendy clothes, while we were just barely getting by. Why couldn't our family get a break? My parents made an honest living – Dada was a correctional officer and Mommy a classroom teacher.

One night, I felt so defeated with life. Dada had recently been laid off from the juvenile detention center. During this period, Mommy was teaching full-time during the days, and had to work as a CNA in the evenings and do assisted living on the weekends. I was too young to get a job but wanted to find a way to help my parents out. Frustrated yet hopeful, I looked to God for answers and some relief. As I released my tear stung prayer into the atmosphere, He transformed my cry into a song that flowed from my pen to God's heart. I was 14 years old when He gave me the first song that I would ever write – *The Light*. This was God's reminder to me that He was and is the ultimate light and would shine on my family's situation.

From that moment on, I walked in the light of God and was determined to illuminate dark places. How can we be light if we don't go into the dark? My parents always reminded us of our commission to be light in dark places. At every high school and college graduation, Mommy dimmed the lights, and played Kathy Troccoli's rendition of "Go Light Your World". As the song played, she lit one candle; we in turn lit one another's candles, and the whole room illuminated with light. This act was symbolic of what they expected us to do with each new achievement. Our degrees were not about us, but rather emphasized the greater impact that we could have on our local and global communities.

Micah 7:7-8
7 – Therefore I will look unto the Lord; I will wait for the God of my salvation: my God will hear me.
8 – Rejoice not against me, O mine enemy: when I fall, I shall arise; when I sit in darkness, the Lord shall be a light unto me.

As a high school student, two instances reminded me that I was operating in the light of God. I attended a Sunday evening service at Greater Palm Bay Church of God, and Pastor Lewinson called me to the altar to stand in proxy for Mommy. As I returned to my seat, Sister Robinson embraced me exclaiming that as Pastor Lewinson was praying, she saw a vision of a star shining over my head. God told her that I was going to be great, but she could not understand why He would give her a revelation about me while I was standing in the gap for my mom. I smiled and squeezed her a little tighter as the song rang out loud in my spirit. She never realized the significance of her words, and has since endearingly referred to me as, "My Star".

The second instance started during my senior year of high school, where I served as an intern in the front office with Mrs. Cordes and Mrs. Unterhorst. During my internship period, I dedicated time in between running daily errands and administrative duties to search for new funding opportunities or write essays for local, state, institutional, and foundational scholarships. It was my goal to get a full scholarship for college and additional funds to cover my living expenses. My three younger siblings were still at home and I wanted to make sure that my college degree would not be a burden on the family. They already made so many sacrifices to get me to this point. I managed to maintain stellar grades throughout high school and was determined to go to college for free. Mrs. Cordes and Mrs. Unterhorst supported my efforts, and so did my guidance counselor Mrs. Christy. During the internship period, I would routinely walk by Mrs. Christy's office to notify me if any new scholarships came in. She shared all opportunities and allowed me to determine my own qualifications and interests.

One day, Mrs. Christy handed me a letter of recommendation to accompany a scholarship application. For some strange reason, I decided not to apply for that scholarship. Later, that year, as I was clearing out some clutter in my dorm room, rummaging through my storage bins and varsity cheerleading bag, I stumbled across the scholarship application and Mrs. Christy's sealed letter. It must have been in God's will because this happened during a point in the semester where I needed a pick-me-up. I rose up off the floor and made my way over to the bed pressing my finger through the envelope to break the seal. I can vividly remember the last line of the letter stating, "Natalie is a star and will shine amongst the brightest and the best!" Those words stirred up something inside of me like fire. It was confirmation of Sister Robinson's dream and the song that God gave me 4 years prior.

No one may have ever seen a star above your head or wrote a letter stating that you will shine amongst the best, but in the greatest love letter written to man, God told us that we are the light of the world and salt of the earth. We were designed to shine and not be hidden. We

Stop minimizing yourself to make others feel comfortable.

ought to stop hiding our light for fear that we will outshine others. God is not calling us to be a part of the crowd, but rather to stand out! So, no matter how hopeless your current situation may seem, dare to shine. The world does not need your lip service talking about the light that you have while it's hidden under a bushel. They just need you to shine. You see, light attracts attention, and so our natural instinct is to dim our light, shrink, and operate at the same level as everyone else for fear of being different or standing out. This is not the season for compromise, light dimming, and blowing out one another's candles. The truth is, there is enough darkness for everyone to shine, and when my light connects with yours...how great is that light! You don't have to dim your light for others to shine; join your light with theirs to produce more light.

> *Matthew 5:16 – Let your light so shine before men, that they may see your good works, and glorify your Father which is in heaven.*

Letting your light shine is just as much about knowing WHO you are as knowing WHOSE you are. You can have the natural glow of God's glory shining through your life. Physical appearance, especially hair, is important to all of us - but especially to adolescents. Hair is often used to

Embrace the natural essence of who you are.

establish and project identity and send a range of messages to those around us. Recently, I decided to transition from a relaxer to wearing my natural hair. I noticed my curls were popping interspersed with some knaps and kinks...all of which made my hair beautiful and unique. Learning how to twist and tease my hair and which products contain ingredients that matched its chemical composition illuminated the beauty. Instead of dreading rainy days for fear of frizziness (as my hair warred against the elements to return to its natural state), I now embraced the moisture with open arms. I experienced a new type of transformation and liberation through my hair because I could finally use my gym membership and exercise without being deterred due to sweat ruining my hairstyles.

During the STEM program, I engaged children in a science lesson focused on Black women's hair. They learned about the harmful effects of hormone-disrupting chemicals in certain hair products. We also discussed humidity and used sensors to measure the water vapor content in the air. Once they began to understand the science behind their hair, students started appreciating their own kinks and curls. They were fascinated by their hair's response to wet or moist air and learned that water is the ultimate moisturizer for their hair type. Spiritually speaking, whenever you are walking in the essence of who God called you to be and what He has called you to do in the earth realm, your light will illuminate the darkest places. You will begin to embrace sweat equity and the external elements as a natural part of the process. We were designed to do great exploits and should cultivate the essence of who we are. Allow God's light to shine through you and His glory to rain on you to expose your natural beauty. Even the *flaws* that you tried to straighten will coil and become beautiful in His sight.

A great responsibility of being the first is to make sure that you're not the last.

In recent years, we are still hearing about the first Black woman to receive a PhD in Astrophysics from Yale University – Jedidah Isler, or the first Black woman to earn a PhD from Massachusetts Institute of Technology (MIT) in nuclear engineering – Mareena Robinson Snowden. We have trailblazers who are courageous enough to endure great hardships in the STEM fields to help pave the way for others. While being the first is a great accomplishment, it carries an even greater responsibility to make sure that you're not the last. This includes engaging in advocacy work, mentoring, and intentional outreach. It is not enough to charter new territory; we have to leave behind instructions and resources to ensure that our successors won't have to slay the same giants.

In learning how to make STEM programing relevant, comprehensive, and accessible, I decided to share my story with others who hope to engage in this type of community-based work. Many times, we invest so much time on being the first, that we often neglect our obligation to pay it forward and make the way easier for others. I can only do so much as one individual; a community is needed as hands and feet on the ground to sustain the work. When you're working against oppressive systems to bridge the divide across communities, institutions, and races to provide equitable learning experiences, there will be resistance. The key is to develop other leaders and create a roadmap that can increase your capacity so that your platform and successes have a greater reach beyond benefitting you. As a trailblazer, you light a torch and are positioned to light a pathway for others to shine. This is how you can leave a lasting legacy!

My youngest son, Angelo, asked me "Mommy what is your favorite color?"

I replied, "I don't know. Maybe red because it looks best on me."

I then asked him the same question, to which he responded, "My favorite color is rainbow."

I paused and pondered how my 4-year old referred to rainbow as if it were just one color. Somehow, I imagined the radiance and beauty that happens when red, orange, yellow, green, blue, indigo, and violet come together to form the visible spectrum. It made me think about the importance of interconnectedness and intergenerational learning – working across disciplines and walks of life to accomplish great feats!

Be visible light in your community.

When we think metaphorically about rainbows and light, we must remember that visibility matters! The visible spectrum is the only part of the electromagnetic spectrum that can be seen with the naked human eye. In addition to creating youth programs that are inclusive and welcoming, we need to be present in schools and even at local football games. It is not just about opening the church doors for people to join us, but also investing that same amount of effort into being engaged in community events. We have to get out of our church buildings in order to build meaningful relationships with various stakeholders – school leaders, business owners, executive directors of non-profit organizations, and those doing grassroots and transformative work. When all of the colors come together, it makes a beautiful masterpiece. So, let's operate on the same wavelength, (scientifically speaking between 380 to 740 nm) to be visible light that can be seen with the human eye. Stay laser focused on the purpose and keep the end in mind.

I share a testimonial from my friend, Natalie, who I met in the very first course of my doctoral program. After having known her for only a few short months, I asked Natalie if she would be interested in serving as an instructor for the STEM program. This interaction took place 7 years ago, and she explains the personal and profound impact of this simple invitation. Natalie sheds light on her approach to becoming more involved, but openly discusses how her decision to join the church family assisted her during some of the toughest moments in her life. I would be remiss not to acknowledge that sometimes life is hard. You will not always be in a position to shine brightly because circumstances have a way of dimming your light. In times like these, you must rely on the light and support of others so that you do not lose your way.

> *"Darkness cannot drive out darkness; only light can do that. Hate cannot drive out hate; only love can do that."*
> **Dr. Martin Luther King Jr.**

Dr. Natalie Marie Khoury Ridgewell, Member, Showers of Blessings Harvest Center, Inc.

I met Dr. Natalie King on the first day of our doctoral program. I immediately noticed her warm smile, joyful laugh, and kindness seemed to naturally radiate from her. We quickly became friends and colleagues, as we noticed that we shared many characteristics, beliefs, and ambitions, and nicknamed ourselves "Natalie ^{Squared}." I had moved away from my home state, family, and friends, save my newly minted husband, and after only a short time in my rigorous program, I realized God had placed Natalie King in my life because he knew I needed her for myriad reasons, both personally and professionally. However, it was not until almost a year later I realized God put her in my life to provide an opportunity for me to grow spiritually.

A few weeks after we had successfully navigated our first year in our academic program, we were sitting in Natalie's office discussing our plans for summer. We both shared a passion for helping others and "giving back," especially to students who had traditionally needed the most support in reaching their highest potential.

Natalie told me about an academic camp – FOCUS that she directed at her church and wanted to know if I was interested in volunteering. I immediately jumped at the opportunity because the students she described who would be attending the camp reminded me of the types of students I had grown up with, and eventually returned to teach, in my home town in rural Georgia. I loved the idea of teaching in an informal learning environment because I thought it would be conducive to being able to get to know children on a more personal and meaningful level, something I consider vital to successfully supporting and meeting their needs.

While both the children and subject area were both similar to whom and what I had previously taught, I knew that a) they did not know that, and b) I had to find a way to relate to them in order to gain their trust and truly engage them in the learning process. Natalie had mentioned that some of the children attended church at Showers of Blessings Harvest Center, Inc. which hosted the camp. I asked if I could attend so that the summer camp participants could see that I was truly invested in them and cared about them beyond our time together in the classroom. I also wanted to have an opportunity for all of us to get to know each other in a more authentic way. I attended a Sunday morning service and invited my husband to accompany me. It was very different from what I, or even he, had experienced in a church before.

As soon as we walked in for the first time, we were immediately welcomed with a loving smile and heartwarming hug. The Church brought more energy and passion than we'd ever experienced. This situation was also unique because we did not look like the rest of the members – we were the only white people in the congregation. Nevertheless, my husband and I felt we had found a new spiritual home. As Dr. Martin Luther King so passionately wished for, we found a place and space in which we felt people were "not judged by the color of their skin but by the content of their character" and "in Christ Jesus [we] are all children of God through faith" (Galatians 3:26).

In my past, God had walked with me through so many hard seasons, from when I was a child into my adulthood. I felt even more blessed to have found a place where I could grow spiritually in ways I never had before through our membership at Showers of Blessings Harvest Center and the wonderful members of that congregation. I certainly never imagined a world where my personal faith and my professional endeavors in academia could co-exist, and Natalie King exemplified how someone could walk and live that life in every way.

Furthermore, I know that nothing on this Earth could have prepared me for the devastating and sudden loss of my dear mother, for the pain and sorrow I faced when the center of my family suddenly disappeared, or the heartache that remains today. I also know that nothing on this Earth except for my steadfast faith in God and His amazing, unyielding, and unconditional love allowed me to survive that season, and certainly not the ones that would continue to follow. The support, love, care, and strengthened faith would not have existed without responding to Natalie's first request to help at the camp.

I believe more than ever that you should always endeavor to live the life God has called you to live and never underestimate the extent to which the impact from giving back to those in need can have not only on a community, but sometimes even on yourself. Jesus died whispering forgiveness on us all, and we cannot claim His mercies without also claiming His practices.

I have also learned how to turn to God and his Grace to find the strength to move forward, even when it seems that it is impossible to do so, as it is His will to fix, mend, redeem, or simply bear witness to whatever happens. Through Him and his unconditional love, even in the darkest of times, I know all things are possible, and I have faith that I will be able to grow, develop, and find beauty, joy, and happiness in whatever season life may bring.

You do not need a pulpit in order to minister.

Many times, we feel as though we are not doing true ministry unless it's behind the pulpit or within the 4 walls of a church building. Ministry happens in our places of employment, the grocery store, at school, and even in our homes. An old proverb talks about charity beginning at home. Learn how to minister to your spouse, children, siblings, and parents before expending your energies on everyone else. Not only do I serve my husband and children and cover them with prayer, but I also help with homework, cook meals, do laundry, and make sure that their needs are taken care of with a spirit of love. This type of ministry requires my simple obedience, time, and expression of love.

In my career as a professor, I minister to students, teachers, my colleagues, and staff. I have an opportunity to be a light in dark places. I can be an example of what the love of Christ should look like...even in The Ivory Tower. The tenure track process can be cut throat and self-seeking, but God has revealed another way that centers <u>service</u>, where He gives wisdom about how to leverage it in my teaching and research. The way in which the system is designed, was not how God intended us to operate. Therefore, He will still give us spiritual strategies and take the foolish things of this world to confound the wise. You do not have to compromise while pursuing your destiny because God orders your steps and illuminates your path.

Pastors should not have to endure the pressures of building up a congregation and community alone. The book of Ephesians talks about the five-fold ministry gifts – apostles, prophets, evangelists, pastors, and teachers. These offices should still be active in contemporary Christian churches. Remember, we are all ambassadors for Christ and have a great responsibility. Stop burying and discounting your gifts. Be the light of the world and salt of the earth. Where is your shine and savor? I dare you to have the impetus and audacity to shine!

Willie and Linda King,
Founders and Pastors of Showers of Blessings Harvest
Center Inc., Gainesville, FL

We have nothing but positive things to say about Natalie and her ability to create programs that captivate the interests of youth. We had faith and a prayer for what we hoped would be a way to serve children in the community and provided her access to a 10,000 square foot building adjacent to our sanctuary and two church vans. She directed a program at the church that really engaged students in science, technology, engineering, and math. Parents appreciated how the program helped their children make academic gains. Many of whom have successfully graduated from high school and are in college. We can speak on a more personal note because one of our granddaughters attended the summer STEM program and weekly tutoring sessions and will be graduating from high school this year. Natalie's love and concern for inner city youth was felt throughout all aspects of the program. She was instrumental in recruiting students, securing partnerships, and applying for small grants and sponsorships.

As pastors, we want to speak to our fellow clergymen and ministers of the gospel, STEM programs expose children to new and exciting career opportunities and hosting them at your church provides a safe and familiar environment for them to explore these subject areas. We were committed to serving African American and minority children who could not afford to pay for these types of experiences elsewhere. We believe that summer and afterschool programs help our children perform at the same level as their peers who do not suffer from poverty and other issues.

In serving as a host site, we learned that certain things must be in place to have a quality program. You must have strong partnerships, engagement of certified teachers, and money to subsidize and offset costs to make it accessible to more children and families. It becomes a difficult task to train individuals who do not have experience in the classroom. You must have the right people in place; certified teachers help your program to grow because parents see the results. Partnerships are also essential for churches who want to host STEM programs, because you cannot sustain these types of programs on your own. Furthermore, if you offer after school programs or have a school, it is easier to host a STEM program because the infrastructure is already in place and gives you a starting point for recruitment. We hosted the program on faith, but it is important to have funds in place to support the needs of the program so that it does not become a burden on the church in the process of helping the community.

We found that STEM programs are very unique from traditional school offerings because students have opportunities to be creative in their learning. Since STEM educates children through the principles of four specific disciplines, it is beneficial to invite experts from each of the areas to participate as well as teachers who are trained in STEM education. Our summer program curriculum served elementary through high school students and infused STEM into the extracurricular activities such as tennis, swimming, cooking, and arts and crafts. Participants received mentoring and tutoring and engaged in exciting field trips. Rich partnerships help make all of this possible through their participation and donations. With technology at an all-time rise, and science being everywhere, we have to find a way to support our children in being innovative and identifying their purpose in this world.

Contemplative Questions:

1) How are you positioned to be a light to others?

   _____

   _____

   _____

   _____

2) In what ways are you positioning yourself to light your world and leave a lasting legacy?

   _____

   _____

   _____

   _____

3) Are you shining the way God intended for you, or is your light hidden?

   _____

   _____

   _____

   _____

4) In what ways can you increase your visibility in the community?

   _____

   _____

   _____

   _____

5) (Insert name here) _____,
   you will shine amongst the brightest and the best!

PRACTICE 5
LEARN HOW TO BE A GOOD STEWARD

Colossians 3:23-24
23 – And whatsoever ye do, do it heartily, as unto the Lord, and not unto men;
24 – Knowing that of the Lord ye shall receive the reward of the inheritance: for ye serve the Lord Christ.

A steward is defined as someone who manages another's property or financial affairs. We have already established that the earth is the Lord's and everything within it. He has given us the responsibility to manage the resources and be good stewards over what He has entrusted to us. The testimonial from Pastors Willie and Linda King is a prime example of how ministers of the gospel can leverage their property and resources to engage in this work and be of service to the community. Churches often have state-of-the-art facilities inclusive of classrooms, office spaces, a sanctuary, fellowship hall, kitchen, gymnasium, computer labs, church vans, and the list goes on. Even the smallest of churches are resource-rich in that they have cultural and social capital within communities. They have a history of providing social services to communities helping to reduce delinquency, crime rates, and drug use in neighborhoods. We can leverage the capital that we possess to address educational inequities.

Be a face that the community can trust!

Concern yourself with the needs of the community and those who are less fortunate. There are children who have big dreams, but harsh realities. The church can serve as a pillar of support within communities by offering tutoring, mentoring, and educational camps and events. Make your presence known in the community! Churches host events and practices during the week, but there is so much more that can be done to maximize the space, especially for youth.

If you are passionate about community engagement and have the capacity to carry out youth development work, start from somewhere. It can be a Saturday program that extends into a summer camp, which can then extend into an afterschool program or school. You must be motivated by the right reasons and willing to make sacrifices and endure the tough seasons to see the fruit of your labor. Consider two R's – reputation and revenue. Churches are usually established as places that people can trust. Once you start offering educational programming, you begin to develop a reputation. If you have a solid curriculum and the right people in place, your reputation will precede you, thus making it easier to secure funds. Investors, foundations, and businesses are always seeking opportunities to get a return on their investments. You need to establish a brand and be a face that the community can trust. The result is that you will spend less time trying to convince people of your value, and more time securing funding and support to carry out your vision. When you become a trusted place for youth programming, it can actually become a revenue generator for your place of worship.

You have to get Buy-In before you can get Benjamins!

Where is the money? High quality programs require an investment and seed funds to operate effectively. It's not impossible to start on faith alone, but you must have a strategic plan in place to grow and sustain your programs. There is always a balancing act of having enough funds to support program activities, while charging a reasonable rate that families can afford. Think of it like buying a car. You have the listing price for the vehicle based on the year, make, and model and a value are determined based on the features. The more money you contribute toward the down payment, the less expensive your monthly payments will be. You determine the value of your program based on the features (field trips, meals, teachers, activities, etc.), then you can estimate how many children you hope to serve, and how much each child will have to pay in order to cover the costs of the program. The more funds you can secure ahead of time to support the program, the more competitive your rates can be for parents. Soon enough, you will not only break even, but will have seed money for the following year. If you stick with the vision, your program has the potential to generate funds to be an additional stream of income for your ministry. While educational programs can provide another source of revenue, it may take a while to make the transition from the red to green. Time, strategy, and support are critical considerations. Furthermore, funding should be secured from multiple methods including fundraising, sponsorships, grants, parental contributions, and assistance programs. Money is not everything but having it sure does help.

Here are some tips on how to secure the Benjamins:

1) ***Fundraising - *** You can begin a fundraising campaign ranging from a community fish fry, hosting a car wash, or even selling Krispy Kreme Doughnuts fundraising certificates and pizza cards. We hosted a summer activities fair for a few years and charged vendors a small entry fee to table and promote their camps and programs. We had bounce houses, food, music, and games with incentives to get parents to attend (such as giveaways for free summer camp, gift cards, and school supplies). This event assisted in raising money for our program and provided an opportunity to attract people to our campus, while exposing them to other summer programs that were happening around the community. Don't forget crowd source funding; this is always an option to get donations through the Internet from people who support the cause.

Fundraising efforts allow people to learn about your programs and vision, while giving them opportunities to contribute financially.

2) **_Sponsorships_** *-* I think of sponsorships a little differently than fundraising. Sponsors are not necessarily getting an item or service in return for their contribution. Organizations and individuals who sponsor are more likely to become a partner and not merely donate. Remember, when you're seeking support, engage your membership first. Then you can garner community support. Your membership should be clear about the vision and mission of the program so that if they are asked about what's happening at the church, they can provide a solid answer. You can have a short presentation about the importance of youth programming and raise a special offering during a service. I also recommend launching a campaign where members can sponsor a child. We used a trifold board and numbered stars 1-75. Each number represented a child and had varying sponsorship levels. Members could choose to sponsor a child for a week of camp, multiple weeks, or even the entire summer. See Appendix 7 for a sample sponsorship request form and Appendix 8 for a sample sponsor letter.

3) **_Grants_** *-* Small local grants are a great start to elicit community support. Think about who is headquartered in your city or county. Are there grant

opportunities offered to support the educational
needs of youth? Are there foundational grants
available? Take the time to see if there are funding
mechanisms in place to offset the costs of running
youth programming.

4) ***Parental Contributions -*** It is critical for parents to
put a little skin in the game and contribute toward
their children's summer enrichment. This must be a
financial investment on behalf of parents to support
a program that is supporting them. If you do not have
grant funds, I recommend charging one flat fee (Ex:
$25 registration fee and $75 per week with a sibling
discount of $10 each child). There will be individuals
who can afford it and pay with ease, and others who
can only afford to pay $25 or $50 per week. The
sponsorships are in place to support those parents so
that the program does not have to assume those costs.
In addition, invite parents to come in and volunteer
or donate snacks such as fruit cups, chips, and juice
boxes. This assists with reducing costs to operate
your program and allows parents an opportunity to
contribute. See Appendix 6 for a sample parent
contribution letter.

5) ***Assistance Programs -*** Every state has assistance
programs where they provide vouchers to families
who meet a certain population of people. There is
typically an income threshold as an eligibility
requirement and provisions for students with special
needs   and   families   who   receive   Temporary

Assistance for Needy Families (TANF) benefits. These vouchers cover a percentage of early head start and school readiness programs. Inquire about the requirements for becoming a provider or approved site. You will need to read closely to ensure that you are able to enact your vision without restrictions or stipulations due to the source of funding. You do not want your curricular creativity to be hindered.

It's commonplace to refrain from talking about money in church. However, you need money and resources to sustain high-quality youth programs. Be careful, because all money is not good money. Do not accept funding that has too many strings attached dictating how it should be spent. You are looking for funds that will support your vision for the program. Assess the needs and resources in your community. Make sure that the price point is not too high where those who need the program cannot afford it, but not too low where those who are working for the program are not compensated for their services. Do not be afraid to fundraise and garner community supporters who share in the same vision.

One way that we were able to serve families who had the greatest needs was through a partnership with the local housing authority. The executive director believed in the mission of the program and secured funding to offset the costs for families who lived in property owned by the housing authority. This partnership was mutually beneficial in that we could support the needs of the program while the housing authority could make summer programming accessible without hosting it. Most importantly, families had an opportunity to enroll their children at a rate they could afford. Think creatively and collaboratively to provide access to extraordinary youth programs.

Pamela Davis, Executive Director of the Gainesville Housing Authority

On behalf of the Gainesville Housing Authority (GHA), we would like to express our great appreciation for Dr. King's efforts and commitment to our residents in providing this exceptional educational experience. GHA has been a partner with I AM STEM since 2016 and I have to say that it has been an absolute pleasure working with I AM STEM and its team members.

In partnership with I AM STEM as well as Caring & Sharing Learning School, GHA residents were able to attend an 8-week summer camp focused on science, technology, engineering, and mathematics with clear and concise learning goals. On top of structured learning, kids also received swimming and tennis lessons as well as a Family Fun Day designed to help families bond with their children. GHA's main focus is aimed at restoring hope for the future in our students. Attracting young minds and capturing their curiosity to ask why and providing the necessary tools to find the answers is a life-changing course of action; which is why we knew this program would give our kids a competitive edge returning back to school. We believed in this program wholeheartedly, therefore, we provided partial scholarships for residents, a fifteen-passenger van for field trips, and became a Diamond sponsor of the program.

Dr. King, GHA would like to express appreciation for your time, treasures, energy and enthusiastic support. We also want to take this opportunity to say a heartfelt "thank you" and provide some feedback from a few parents over the years.

Ms. Tamesha (Parent) - My kids loved the program. They enjoyed the interactive lessons most of all. I would definitely recommend this program to other families.

Ms. Alicia (Parent) - My son absolutely enjoyed every second of this program. Some days I couldn't even get him to leave. The teaching skills were beyond expected; my son was able to quickly transition to the next grade level.

Ms. Octavia (Parent) - My child absolutely loved every second of the program. She missed no days and I have to say she learned a lot of information at the age of 4. She loves science so much now. I would like to thank everyone at I AM STEM and Caring and Sharing.

Ms. Ashley (Parent) - My children usually hate attending any school during the summer, but they loved this program. I plan to have them in this program every summer. Thanks to all the teachers that helped my kids.

Proverbs 23:4 – Labor not to be rich: cease from thine own wisdom.

Access to vans are a staple for STEM programs because it's beneficial for students to travel off-campus to visit research laboratories, go fishing, do nature walks at local parks, or even visit a botanical garden or museum. When you have access to your own vehicles like church vans, you can cover the insurance, maintenance, fuel, and a stipend for the driver (who you will probably hire as a staff member for the camp). This is much more efficient than paying for a school bus or coach bus every time you want to go on a field trip. If you are in partnership with a school district, it may be possible to request use of a school bus during the summer, and hire a district approved driver.

Kingdom work requires kingdom thinking!

You have to sow a seed in order to reap a harvest. The question is, how much are you willing to invest? How many seeds are you willing to sow and are you taking care of the ground in which the seeds are being planted? Leverage the expertise of your membership but be open to bringing in support from the community in areas where you may be lacking. Include parents in the decision-making process. Ask them to recommend teachers who were effective with their children and invite them to participate in your programs. We cannot neglect the business aspect of operating faith-based institutions and must generate enough revenue to keep the church doors opened. In serving the needs of others, the needs of the church can be met. When we assist children in meeting their educational and career goals, they can change the trajectory of their families, becoming the next engineers, academics, and scientists who are now tithe payers. Our community changes when we invest in the futures of our youth.

Be alert about initiatives that are taking place in your community. Look at the vision and mission of local organizations, because you could be meeting one of their missions or strategic goals simply by partnering with them. Do away with competitions and being territorial; remember, this is kingdom work designed to bring God glory. There are churches and organizations that have no desire to start their own program or reinvent the wheel. They would rather partner with an organization that already has programming in place and has built strong connections and relationships with the community they hope to serve. They understand their inability and possible ineffectiveness in trying to address these issues alone and seek partnerships to engage with authenticity. They are able to contribute to the cause in ways that are solicited and needed rather than trying to figure it out on their own which can often lead to unintentional consequences and harm. I have learned that many churches want to become engaged in addressing systemic issues and do not know where to start.

Educational youth programs, particularly those that focus on the STEM disciplines, is one approach that I have found to be effective.

Dr. Joanne LaFramenta, Co-chair, Social Justice Committee, United Church of Gainesville, Gainesville, FL

During March 2016, the United Church of Gainesville (UCG) hosted a community symposium to discuss racial disparities and social justice issues in our community. This symposium ignited a call-to-action for members of the congregation. We actively solicited connections with community organizations whose members lived on the east side of town. We hoped to foster connections between individuals across racial and socioeconomic lines so that we could interact in ways that recognized the dignity and cultural contributions of each group of people.

At this time, Dr. King and I shared an office at the University of Florida. As she shared details of her work, I wanted my fellow church members to learn more. This was exactly the type of opportunity that could allow us to share our blessings and forge relationships across races. The Social Justice Committee invited Dr. King to make a presentation during our worship service. Her appeal delighted the congregation and affirmed our hopes for a partnership with a group primarily serving Black residents of Gainesville and Alachua County.

Over the last three years, UCG has contributed to the needs of I AM STEM Camp. Professionals have opened the doors to their labs and offices to share their work with young people. Members have volunteered during the summer program exposing youth to their careers in medicine and the STEM disciplines. We have also provided financial support to this noteworthy program. Children for which we have provided sponsorships have shared their experiences with us by inviting us to the culminating ceremonies and writing letters of thanks. We value this partnership as a friendship between associations seeking to address racial disparities and inequities in our community.

Contemplative Questions:

1) If you are currently offering youth programs, how are these programs being funded?

_____

_____

_____

_____

_____

2) What organizations or businesses may be good partners or supporters of a STEM program for youth?

_____

_____

_____

_____

_____

3) Are there greater systemic or social justice issues that can be solved through meaningful partnerships? If so, explain.

_____

_____

_____

_____

PRACTICE 6
YOUR GIFTS WILL MAKE ROOM FOR YOU

James 1:17 – Every good gift and every perfect gift is from above, and cometh down from the Father of lights, with whom is no variableness, neither shadow of turning.

This practice focuses on how you use the gifts that God has bestowed upon you. I am reminded about the parable of the talents found in Matthew 25:14-30, where a master is preparing to travel, and entrusts his property with three servants. He distributes talents based on their abilities and gives one servant five talents, another two talents, and the last servant one talent. Each talent is representative of a significant amount of money. Upon the master's return, they gave a report regarding their efforts and productivity. The servant who had five talents, traded and gained an additional five talents. The second servant followed suit and doubled his talents as well. The last servant with one talent was fearful that he would lose his master's money and chose to bury it. While he referred to the other two servants as good and faithful, he called the last servant "wicked and slothful". Even if that servant put the talent in the bank, it would have at least accrued interest over time. The master took that talent away and gave it to the servant with ten talents. I will liken your talents to the gifts that

God has entrusted you with while in the earth realm. My question to you is, what have you done with your talents?

Your gifts have the potential to open doors!

Proverbs 18:16 – A man's gift maketh room for him, and bringeth him before great men.

The Holy Bible promises that your gifts will make room for you. No matter how small you think your gift is, it can open up supernatural doors to a fully financed college education, successful career, or even a thriving business. Do not focus on your inadequacies, but rather shift your focus on what you can do effortlessly (as an individual and as an organization). You can leverage these gifts to design high quality programs. What do you have in your hand? You have the rod of God, so use it! He has given you a powerful assignment that you cannot accomplish in your own strength. What words has God given you to speak? Let Him teach you what you shall say.

Exodus 4:2 – And the Lord said to him, What is that in thine hand? And he said, A rod.
Exodus 4:10 – And Moses said unto the Lord, O my Lord, I am not eloquent, neither heretofore, nor since thou hast spoken unto thy servant: but I am slow of speech, and of a slow of tongue.

We can always come up with excuses for why we cannot accomplish our God-given assignment. Many times, our excuses are quite valid because they are based on our current realities. Moses was honest when he reminded the Lord that he had a speech impediment. God is so gracious; He comforted Moses by instructing him to go because He would teach Moses what to say. We may not have the most eloquent way of communicating our thoughts, but God will endow our words and direct us on what to speak. The keyword to remember is "GO". The enemy comes to steal, kill, and destroy your name, reputation and legacy. What are you doing with this information? What is your response? Do you lock yourself in a room, tuck your tail, and quit, or do you square up and get in the fight? This is the season to engage, and fight like your children's lives, and children's children's lives depend on it. You have the power to generate wealth, and now is not the time to bury your talents. If you will have enough faith to use your gifts and invest your talents, God will give the increase.

There is a misconception that you have to wait until after you've accomplished your own goals to assist others. The reality is that you refine your gifts through service, mentorship, and teaching. I share a testimonial from an aspiring teacher, Candace, who served as an intern for I AM STEM Camp. Candace did not have prior classroom teaching experiences but used her passion for students and expertise in science and technology to formulate powerful lessons that made a tremendous impact. We partnered with an institution of higher education to become an approved internship site for their teacher candidates. They awarded Candace with a stipend and gave her access to resources, while we provided a space for her to engage authentically with children and the larger community. As a college student, her gift to teach STEM subjects was sharpened through her mentorship of high school students. Candace personally benefited from this experience by developing skill sets that are critical to becoming a highly effective teacher.

Candace Weiss, I AM STEM Intern, University of Florida Noyce Program, Gainesville, FL

Last summer, I had the pleasure of collaborating with Dr. Natalie King who provided me with an opportunity to teach a class of high school students at I AM STEM Camp. My main goal was to expose them to new knowledge, encourage their pursuits of college and careers, and engage them academically. To accomplish this, I thoroughly planned daily interactive lessons, purchased experiment supplies, organized guest speakers, arranged to borrow iPads from UF's College of Education, and conducted teacher interviews to gain teaching advice. To create my lessons, I drew from my high school experience, online ideas, and student interests. We practiced ACT and SAT questions, engaged in STEM driven activities, exercised writing skills, built resumès, and participated in educational field trips. Since I plan to become an educator, this was a perfect opportunity to refine my teaching philosophy and gain real world experience.

I received a stipend through UF's College of Education Noyce Program to serve as an intern for I AM STEM Camp. This contribution provided human capital while keeping the cost at a minimum for the students. Overall, I am extremely grateful to have been a part of I AM STEM Camp. This internship has certainly changed my teaching philosophy. While I assumed teaching would be an innate skill, I realize now that most excellent teachers have to work hard to become excellent. In my mind, I always felt like it would come naturally to me, but in practice, I realized the depth of knowledge and confidence that teaching requires.

Another valuable skill that I gained was the ability to distinguish learning styles among students. In the past, I assumed that each student learned best the way that I do – through interactive activities, moving around the room, and connecting with other students. In contrast, I realized that some students preferred learning through experimentation and valued individual projects that they could share with their peers. This eight-week experience provided me with an opportunity to recognize these differences, adjust my teaching style, and try various teaching approaches to keep students engaged.

Possibly the most significant lesson that I learned was that I may not always have a tremendous impact on every student, but I must still try. I can focus on the small positive changes and embrace every opportunity to become a better educator for the next student that I encounter.

Additionally, I added multiple new lessons to my teaching toolbox and updated my UFTeach website to include eight weeks of rigorous lesson planning. While not every day was easy, my experience teaching at I AM STEM Camp has prepared me for entering into my first year of teaching with a persevering and confident mindset.

Churches need to be solutions-driven and not religion-driven.

The world is becoming more advanced and the STEM disciplines can assist in opening doors. We are now faced with the challenge of preparing students for futuristic careers – ones we don't even know exist. Are churches a part of the equation and conversation? In what ways are faith-based institutions helping children find and nurture their gifts? When parents are looking for extracurricular activities and summer programs that promote academic engagement during the summer months, are they enrolling their children in faith-based programs? Churches typically provide competitive rates for out-of-school programs, but many do not have the capacity to offer cutting edge curriculum. Countless educators and professionals are members of churches and typically work for and support other programs, rather than seeing their own church home as a viable place to invest their gifts, talents, and time. Let's not get caught up in denominations and religion, but rather solutions for our communities. The Church needs to have a seat at the table in these critical conversations because churches are deeply embedded centers of culture within communities. I am specifically interested in working with faith-based institutions to build their capacity to reimagine and expand the horizons of STEM education. We can help children realize their gifts and true potential by engaging them in solutions-driven approaches to community issues, which promotes STEM for social justice. The Church can teach children how to be functional in the 21st century and create their own opportunities.

Whole child development is key to gift manifestation.

In this season, the Church must take a stand and BE PRESENT not passive. We have work to do and a critical role to play in building the Kingdom of God and mitigating social and educational disparities. It is our responsibility to make sure that children have access to exciting careers, but also new ways of thinking, creating, and being. I briefly talked about the importance of whole child development in Chapter 2 and focused on embedding the spiritual aspect into our youth programs. I allude back to whole child development here because the only way their gifts will be manifested is if their needs are met. We need to develop youth who are socially, emotionally, intellectually, culturally, mentally, and spiritually sound!

Churches typically provide opportunities for children to participate in performing arts during the weekly services (which I certainly appreciate), but it often does not translate into the way children are being assessed in their formal schools. Micah can sing, but can he spell? Susie can dance, but can she divide? It's all about having balance and setting up our children for success in all aspects of their lives. If they are not successfully passing their classes in school, it leaves a deep void and an opportunity for the Church to play a vital role. Children's Church and Vacation Bible School (VBS) are a start, but the structure oftentimes is limiting. Let's redefine what engagement looks like by engaging the mind and tapping into children's true gifts by giving them a new and critical view on

Thou shalt walk in thy purpose.

life. Let's expose our youth to a world that they have neither seen nor experienced, by getting them into the community to visit local parks and outside of their communities for college tours. Youth must learn how to think for themselves and need to unlearn that every problem can be solved by simply filling in a bubble. We can also help to replace defeated mindsets with ones of victory by changing the "I can't" to "I can" or at the very least, "I'll try".

When we walk in our purpose unapologetically and with authenticity, we give youth permission to do the same. We have to plant the seeds, water them, and allow God to bring the increase. If we are not careful, the House of God can serve to perpetuate oppression rather than provide a space for liberation. We spend a lot of time focusing on what "thou shalt not" do instead of the affirmative. What actions should children be engaging in to replace undesired and damaging behaviors? When we are teaching children that they should not steal, we should implement financial literacy lessons. We need to encourage them to become entrepreneurs and have multiple streams of income, while teaching them strategies on how they can prevent living from paycheck to paycheck and owning their own properties instead of renting. We can offer incentive programs that support this kind of thinking rather than emphasizing benevolence funds.

Churches have the capacity to teach self-sufficiency rather than reliance on prayers for a miracle to meet their basic needs every week. The poor will be among us always, but the people of God were not designed to "rob Peter to pay Paul". The bible teaches us the essence of entrepreneurship and how to live prosperous lives. Our children should have the mindset that they will be lenders and not borrowers. They need to understand the importance of good credit before they have a poor credit score and learn the bondage of credit cards and student loan debt before they've signed their lives over to Chase and Sallie Mae. We can teach them how to live within their means and what financial freedom looks and feels like. It's not about having the latest cars, while struggling to make the monthly payments. Most of all, we can teach our children the importance of giving and not just receiving, because God is a God of multiplication. They have to sow in order to reap a harvest. These are lessons that often never get taught in church. If programs are available, it is for adults and often neglects to serve the youth. We have scriptures to back us up and need to find innovative ways to reach this generation beyond religion and spiritual needs so that they can become productive citizens in society.

To close this chapter, I share a testimonial from a teacher in I AM STEM Camp, and how her gifts made room for her to help sustain STEM programming for youth within our community. Mrs. Wanda Lloyd launched an organization based on her passion for dance, but the fruit of her obedience is serving a far greater purpose.

Mrs. Wanda Lloyd, I AM STEM Teacher & Founder of BLSSD Future

In 2012, I was informed about an opportunity to enrich children's lives during the summer months. From that moment until now, I AM STEM Camp has been the highlight of my summer breaks. The first year I worked with Mrs. Natalie King, I knew our relationship would be GOLDEN. She had a level of trust that allowed me to SOAR (Shape Our Academic Realm) with the children that we served. Mrs. Natalie allowed me to be me – energetic, creative, and loud! I had no problem getting and keeping the children's attention, and she has strategically placed me with 4th-6th grade students each year. I started with her when she directed FOCUS Summer Program at the church to I AM STEM Camp at a local school.

Because of the passion she brought to the program, she attracted other educators with the same zeal for teaching children BEYOND THEIR LIMITS, which is why I wanted my son to attend with me as a 4-year-old. I paid the tuition at his center so that he would not lose his spot for the school year but brought him to the camp to be exposed to the comprehensive and exciting curriculum. The amount of knowledge that the kindergarten teacher poured into my son at that time made him more than ready for kindergarten the following year. He has attended the summer camp every summer since.

Because teaching the whole child is important to Mrs. Natalie, it didn't surprise me that she allowed me to implement BLSSD Future as an extracurricular activity. BLSSD (Ballroom, Line Dance, Swing Out, and Steppin' Dancers) Future is a dance program for youth, teaching the basics of urban ballroom, soul line dance, DFW swing out, and Chicago style steppin dance styles. I was really impressed by how quickly the students fell in love with dancing, especially because they had to hold hands. I had previously taught my homeroom class during the formal school year, and so I felt the dance curriculum could be shortened and used to prepare the summer scholars for a dance performance at the culminating ceremony. Their dance went viral on Facebook and everyone applauded the children's performance. However, I wanted people to recognize the excellent program that made this all possible!

In June of 2017, I organized the 1st Annual "Teach Me to Dance" Interactive Workshop and Fundraiser was going to take place to highlight the academic learning of our children *as well as being introduced to the art of dance. It was my vision to raise money to ensure that more children are being reached by an awesome program focusing on Science, Technology, Engineering and Math. I had no idea what to truly expect but was hoping that dance groups from across the nation would travel to Gainesville, FL, to support this great effort. That is exactly what happened! All forms of communication revealed the purpose of the fundraiser and that the proceeds would benefit I AM STEM Camp. In 2017, over $3,200 was raised after all expenses, and in 2018, over $5,000 was raised that went toward supporting families to send their children to camp.*

I feel so blessed to have the opportunity to work with such a beautiful spirited woman like Natalie King. She has allowed me to combine my love for dance with my passion to see children achieve academic success. I AM STEM will always be supported by BLSSD Future as long as I have breath in my body and Natalie King giving new vision and insights into promoting academic excellence for our children.

Contemplative Questions:

1) What gifts have God given to you?

   _____

   _____

   _____

   _____

2) What are some excuses or limitations that have prevented you from investing your all and sharing those gifts with others?

   _____

   _____

   _____

   _____

3) How are you using your gifts to give God glory?

   _____

   _____

   _____

   _____

4) Do you have innovative ideas about how to make STEM education more accessible within your community (even if you do not have a background in the STEM disciplines or education)?

   _____

   _____

   _____

   _____

PRACTICE 7
LET EVERYTHING BE DONE DECENTLY AND IN ORDER

I Corinthians 14:40 - Let all things be done decently and in order.

What does it mean for everything to be done decently and in order? This chapter focuses on how to develop programs with the spirit of excellence. As you offer educational youth programs, do not be so quick to cut corners. I heard a quote that there is no shortcut to success. In fact, it's the process that teaches you how to effectively manage and grow extraordinary programs.

It's not about intention, but rather reception!

How do people perceive and receive the work that you are doing? Many times, we have the right intentions, but it's received the wrong way. In previous chapters, I discussed the importance of introspection as well as listening to the community to hear their needs. Remember to develop relationships with the community in which you are serving and ensure that open lines of communication exist. Another important consideration is representation. If you do not live in that particular neighborhood, invite residents to have a seat at the table as decision-makers. The leadership of the program should include some familiar faces, because they are critical to the success of your program and their input is invaluable. Respect and honor the cultural resources of those individuals.

People are often hesitant to engage with individuals whose realities are different from their own, for fear that they will be rejected or cause harm rather than good. Turning a deaf ear is convenient but not a suitable answer. We must move beyond simply tolerating one another and seek to understand one's culture and lived experiences. For effective partnerships, our programs should offer solutions to community issues that embrace its cultural wealth and resources. Try to identify with people and their struggles. Everyone cannot *pull themselves up by their bootstraps* because there are systemic structures in place that maintain the current social order. We have to be bold enough to disrupt forms of oppression even if it means relinquishing some of our own privilege in the process. This is how we will ensure that our programs are not only extraordinary but will meet the community needs and be well-received.

Remember, there are rich resources even within communities that are labeled as impoverished or dysfunctional. Leverage the historical and cultural knowledge of matriarchs and patriarchs and combine it with the contemporary and innovative ideas of youth. Do not perpetuate the savior complex by waiting on people and businesses to come into your communities to enact change. Dust off your cape, because you are the superhero for which your community is searching. Trust that you know what's best and can establish partnerships that will provide the most appropriate programs for children and their families. Once you identify resources that exist within your own community, then you can collaborate with surrounding organizations, businesses, and institutions to further develop the programs to make them more robust. Do not give up your rights and influence to outside entities. Set parameters and organize how they will participate in reasonable and meaningful ways. This approach provides a safeguard against the unintended consequences of individuals who may mean well but impose their own agendas on your program. There are visionaries who reside in your community with the necessary talents, skill sets, and intellectual capabilities. Furthermore, I encourage you to support small local businesses, and do not be afraid to circulate money within your community for added fiscal security and development. What are you waiting for? Start a grassroots movement and work collectively to enact social change. Your communities and places of worship can become storehouses filled with resources and wealth. Extraordinary programs take time and careful attention to detail. Your program's success is dependent upon your ability to continuously improve and not see your efforts as a finished product, but rather a work in progress.

Ephesians 3:20-21
20 – Now unto him that is able to do exceedingly abundantly above all that we ask or think, according to the power that worketh in us,
21 – Unto him be glory in the church by Christ Jesus throughout all ages, world without end. Amen.

Extraordinary programs require preparation and action. If it were easy, everyone would be doing it. You must be willing to put your hands to the plow and invest the time, resources, and energy to develop and sustain your programs. Once you begin to feed your faith and step outside of your

comfort zone, just stand in expectancy because God will bless and reward you. He opens up doors that no man can shut!

Feed your faith, starve your fears!

When the blessings begin to pour out, do not forget to remain humble. Show your gratitude and give God all of the glory. Remember, we are simply willing vessels carrying out His work in the earth realm. Rethink your approach and level of community involvement. You have the capacity to do more than what you are doing and need to operate at a greater level of faith. This may require you to cut away some things and people. There must be unity and one sound, which is preceded by great leadership and a clear vision. You will need to exercise your faith and chase after the vision to overcome those moments of doubt and fear.

II Corinthians 12:9 – And he said unto me, my grace is sufficient for thee: for my strength is made perfect in weakness. Most gladly therefore will I rather glory in my infirmities, that the power of Christ may rest upon me.

There is just something about God's amazing grace! He makes provision, and His unlimited strength is made perfect in your weakness. Oftentimes, people see your accomplishments and despise you, or even try to impersonate you. They desire the outcome without having gone through the process. I realize that not everyone is graced to engage in this type of work. It reminds me of the teaching profession which often does not get the respect it deserves in our society. Even some of the most successful

Grace makes all the difference.

businessmen, influencers, and professionals do not have the skills to effectively lead a classroom or wear the many hats of teachers. When you offer programs, take pride in the personalized touch that you bring, which can only be imitated not duplicated. God gives you the grace to offer extraordinary programs. As you begin thinking about your specific role, note that there are individuals who will work directly with children and their families, others who will work behind the scenes to ensure that logistics are taken care of, and yet others who may never step foot on your property, and provide donations and financial support. Make your programs unique to you and God will give you the grace and wisdom to sustain the work. He'll put the right people in your path to help meet all of your programmatic needs.

I Corinthians 15:10 – But by the grace of God I am what I am: and His grace which was bestowed upon me was not in vain; but I labored more abundantly than they all: yet not I, but the grace of God which was with me.

Be intentional and strategic about your community efforts and gain comfort in knowing that your partners, leadership team, and even staff will change overtime. When your vision is clear, the essence of the program will be preserved even through transitions. I had to learn that being nice does not build good programs. People want structure and order, knowing that they can depend on you to deliver what you promised. I was always pleasant and respectful, but most of all, I made sure that they could count on my word and the quality of program they would receive. Be upfront with parents and children about your expectations, and then follow through. Stay up-to-date with records and have a checks and balances system in place to ensure accuracy. Communicate frequently with families so that they are aware of activities and events. Parents are more likely to trust you with their children if they can trust you on your word.

Everything about your program should exude the spirit of excellence – from the flyers and websites, to the way that people are greeted when they walk in the door. They should feel the love of Jesus Christ in all aspects of your program. I share a brief overview of areas that need attention to promote safety and minimize risks.

1. ***Organization* -** There is nothing that drives people crazier than a disorganized program. While I believe in children having a level of freedom, there has to be proper supervision and protocols in place to ensure their safety. Children should not be running around aimlessly in confined spaces unless it is a part of a lesson (like a science activity about entropy or states of matter where students are personifying gas molecules). Provide opportunities for play in open spaces utilizing age-appropriate equipment. Chaos should not be the daily norm. Your program will not last long if no one seems to know what's going on or have answers to parents' questions. Spend time crafting your organizational structure and create a clear schedule that is visible and available to everyone. Teachers and staff need to know what children are doing at all times, and parents should be aware of when their children will be on/off campus as well as what they are learning. Most times when children go home, they share the last thing that they did for that day. They'll get in the car and say, "Mom, we watched a movie today", when they watched a movie for the last thirty minutes waiting until their parents arrived. You can teach children how to tell parents about their day by having opportunities for reflection before they leave. Not

only will this assist with giving a fuller picture of what was accomplished, but you can also assess whether or not your learning goals were met. See Appendix 1 for a sample calendar overview and Appendix 2 for a sample lesson plan template.

2. ***Procedures*** - In thinking about organization, it is essential to have procedures in place. What happens if there is a medical emergency? What is the procedure if a fire starts in the kitchen? What system are you using for parents to check their children in and out? Do you have a procedure for off-campus field trips? Are there uniformed shirts so that children and teachers can be easily identified? Some procedures require us to simply get back to the basics. Start with simple routines and remain consistent. For example, children should know that there are swimming lessons on Mondays and Wednesdays and tennis lessons on Tuesdays and Thursdays. This will help them to dress appropriately and remember to bring change of clothes on swimming days. If you are in charge, come early and ensure that the space is ready. Instead of having ground rules, work with children to co-develop camp norms that specify expectations and proper behaviors for all parties. Before you launch your programs, familiarize yourself with federal, state, county, and city regulations to ensure that you maintain compliance. Your facilities will likely need to undergo environmental health and fire inspections unless you apply for exemptions. There may be additional stipulations and regulations if you are serving children who are younger than five years old. Keep all of

this in mind as you identify, evaluate, and prioritize risks for running programming.

3. ***Open communication with parents* -** Parents should have a systematic way of finding out information. You can update your website, send out weekly newsletters, or use email and text correspondence. It's important to offer multiple options for parents to receive information. You can also subscribe to classroom communication apps such as Remind or Class Dojo to share photos, track student engagement, or send updates in real time. Although these methods of communication are useful, they should not replace face-to-face interactions with parents. Have meaningful and regular conversations with parents and offer resources that they can use to support their children at home. If you notice that their child is struggling with multiplication, print out a few handouts or even purchase a set of flashcards so that they can practice at home. A signature event that we host annually is a Make n Take Night, where we invite parents to share in their children's education. They receive strategies on how to facilitate STEM activities and assist their children with homework. We present each parent with a passport that gets stamped as they progress from one station to the next. Sample activities range from engaging them in questions and sentence starters that they can use to assist their children in synthesizing and comprehending what they have read. Some mathematics activities include geometric Tetris, measurements, and skip counting songs they can play at home to teach the fundamentals of multiplication. They also learn about the engineering

design process through competitions where they team up as a family to design solutions to a problem. Earlier in the book, I discussed the importance of administering evaluation surveys and facilitating focus groups to receive feedback from parents to inform future iterations of your program. This is an opportunity to engage all stakeholders in a reflection of their experiences - what went well and what could be improved. See Appendix 4 for a sample passport from Make N Take Night and Appendix 5 for a sample evaluation form.

4. *__Professional Development (PD)__* - All individuals, from the executive director(s) to teachers and staff, need to receive opportunities for professional learning where they can understand the vision of the program and how they fit into that overall vision. Your team will have varying levels of expertise and individuals who work across disciplines. PD allows you to foster community while learning best practices. Seek out teacher educators and STEM professionals who can engage you as learners while modeling your prospective roles as facilitators. You do not need someone to lecture you about what to do, but rather an individual who can provide an experience of what it looks and feels like. Before making an investment to fly in *world renowned experts* for a one-shot experience, exhaust your local resources first. Remember the importance of leveraging the social and cultural capital that exists within your community. There are professionals and educational researchers who look like the children being served and have the heart and specialized knowledge to bring about change. Sustained

PD is extremely beneficial because it takes time to improve pedagogical practices and learn content. Once the logistics are in place for the camp with flyers in schools, applications available for registration, and teaching staff identified and hired, I recommend that you organize a targeted PD workshop a few weeks prior to starting your program. This time should be dedicated to designing curricular activities, organizing classes based on who is registered, planning and testing out lessons and investigations, purchasing supplies, and hosting an orientation for parents and children. Even if you are only offering short-term programming, opportunities for professional learning should still be year-round. Do not be afraid to incorporate samples of students' projects and other program artifacts into your PD to receive feedback and discuss successes and missed opportunities. Plan field trips to visit local museums or informal science institutions as a method of professional learning. In addition to providing PD that attends to programmatic and curricular needs, incorporate issues of diversity, equity, and inclusivity. This can range from local disparities that everyone can explore like access to equitable education and medical services, to national and international trends related to underrepresentation in the STEM fields.

5. ___Curriculum -___ The vision for science education is rapidly changing with goals of increasing students' academic rigor by applying scientific and engineering practices with core ideas and crosscutting concepts to deepen their understanding of science regardless of the background

(NRC, 2012; NGSS Lead States, 2013). We are exploring how to make science more accessible to and inclusive of all groups of students. Rhetoric is moving away from "The Scientific Method" to engaging students in 8 practices that are characteristic behaviors of scientists and engineers:

    i.   Asking questions (for science) and defining problems (for engineering)

    ii.   Developing and using models

    iii.   Planning and carrying out investigations

    iv.   Analyzing and interpreting data

    v.   Using mathematics and computational thinking

    vi.   Constructing explanations (for science) and designing solutions (for engineering)

    vii.   Engaging in argument from evidence

    viii.   Obtaining, evaluating, and communicating information

There are also 8 standards for mathematical practice that were released by the National Governors Association (2010). These Common Core State Standards (CCSS) have been adopted by many states and require students to:

    i.   Make sense of problems and persevere in solving them

    ii.   Reason abstractly and quantitatively

    iii.   Construct viable arguments and critique the reasoning of others

    iv.   Model with mathematics

    v.   Use appropriate tools strategically

    vi.   Attend to precision

vii.   Look for and make use of structure
viii.   Look for and express regularity in repeated reasoning

Furthermore, Common Core State Standards (CCSS) for English Language Arts (ELA) emphasize literacy across the subject areas and college and career readiness. Children are required to think critically and analytically to solve problems. They are also expected to practice regularly with complex texts and academic language. Their reading, writing, and speaking should be grounded in evidence from literary and informational texts where they build knowledge through content-rich nonfiction.

In addition to ELA, mathematics, and science standards, there are two additional sets of standards that can be leveraged to design transformative lessons. The Southern Poverty Law Center (2016) released Social Justice Standards to promote anti-bias education across grade levels. These standards focus on prejudice reduction and collective action through 4 domains – identity, diversity, justice, and action. You may freely access the framework using the following website – https://www.tolerance.org/frameworks. The International Society for Technology in Education provides technology standards as a framework for students, educators, and administrators to rethink education and create more innovative learning environments. These standards can be found at www.iste.org/standards and emphasize digital literacy, innovative design, computational thinking, knowledge construction, global collaboration, creative communication, and students becoming empowered learners.

I will not delve too deeply into the standards and practices because some states have adopted the NGSS and CCSS, while others have created their own. What I will emphasize is the level of thinking that students are expected to do at younger and younger ages. We have the potential to help children develop these skills during out-of-school time to promote their success in school. We can make our curriculum relevant by promoting multicultural education and social responsibility, where our programs do not focus solely on remediation, but rather on enrichment through comprehensive curriculum.

Comprehensive curriculum not only prepares students for the next grade level, but for life. I encourage you to start with a social justice theme that is initiated by a community problem. For example, participants can explore how schools serve contradictory roles – empowering and liberating certain populations while marginalizing and oppressing others. Infuse history, current events, and even politics in the conversation, because the past helps us to understand and problematize the present in order to encourage progress for generations to come. Partner with educators who can assist with creating standards-aligned lessons and engage community organizations for relevant experiential learning. Children should be afforded opportunities to ask difficult questions, propose solutions, and take action through civic engagement and advocacy. If you are offering a camp, it is helpful to have one clear theme that spans across the length on your program so that there is alignment in terms of disciplinary content and selected field trips. Table 1 presents an example of a 5-week program with a sustainability theme and sample activities for each week. I listed a few science and engineering practices that correspond with the learning goals. Can you think of ways to embed any other standards and practices?

Table 1. Sample STEM Learning Activities

Sustainability Theme	Sample Activities	Learning Goals	Science/Engineering Practices
Recycling and Composting	Visit a local transfer facility	* Scholars will learn about the recycling program in their community. * Scholars will discuss the advantages of recycling locally and the global impacts of their actions.	Asking questions (for science) and defining problems (for engineering) Obtaining, evaluating, and communicating information
Clean Water	Visit a local fishery	* Scholars will learn about the movement of water on earth and test the water quality. * Scholars will learn about invasive and native Florida species and explore 4 different endangered species of sturgeon in the aquaculture facilities.	Analyzing and interpreting data Using mathematics and computational thinking Developing and using models
Organic Gardening	Plant growth investigations	* Scholars will conduct investigations to determine factors that affect plant growth. * Scholars will design experiments and identify the dependent and independent variables and control. * Scholars will redesign their investigations based on the results and provide rationale for each revision.	Planning and carrying out investigations Analyzing and interpreting data Using mathematics and computational thinking
Green Energy	Energy Charades	* Scholars will learn about different types of energy sources: non-renewable energy sources (fossil fuels) and renewable energy sources, such as, geothermal energy, solar energy, wind energy, hydroelectric energy or biomass energy.	Obtaining, evaluating, and communicating information
Pollution	Modeling water pollution	* Scholars will identify sources of water pollution and design solutions to help mitigate the program.	Asking questions (for science) and defining problems (for engineering) Developing and using models Planning and carrying out investigations

6. *Meals -* One aspect of the program that cannot be an afterthought is how you are going to feed children. During my first year serving as an onsite director, we purchased food items and paid staff members a stipend to prepare breakfast, lunch, and snacks each day. This approach was simply not sustainable and consumed much of our budget. In subsequent years, we partnered with meal programs offered through the school district and a local food bank to offset meal costs. Also consider offering an elective where children learn how to make simple and healthy snacks. You can embed health and nutrition into the curriculum by teaching children how to grow their own fruits and vegetables and hosting cooking demonstrations. This can be accomplished by starting an organic garden to promote a greater awareness of where their food comes from, as well as healthier food options that avoid synthetic pesticides.

7. *Fiscal Responsibility -* It is helpful to run your program under a 501(c)(3) nonprofit organization because donors can write off their contributions. Make sure that you keep good financial records. Organize all receipts, scan them, and store them in a secure space. The summer program account should be handled separately from the operating account. You need a team that can reconcile transactions, deposits, and categorize spending. After the program has ended, parents and sponsors should receive a contribution statement with the amount they contributed, the tax identification number, and an invitation to donate again for the following year. Make a practice of creating end-of-year reports that share information related to how

many children were served; demographics related to race/ethnicity, gender, class, and grade level; and highlight student achievements and teacher contributions. Provide opportunities for children to write thank you letters to sponsors sharing their experiences. Donors like to know how their contributions were used and if they are getting a return on their investments. Most of all, have a checks and balances system and do everything with integrity.

Cover your program with more than just prayer.

You need to be the source of reliability and not liability. As you launch and grow STEM education programs for youth, make sure that proper insurance coverages are in place. Anything that can happen, will happen, and so you need to prepare for the unexpected. Even with the best procedures in place, accidents or emergencies are inevitable. Purchase liability insurance and practice being preventative over reactionary! If you are transporting children off-campus for any reason, make sure that you have appropriate car insurance in place to cover the vehicles, allowing only drivers who are on the policy to operate those vehicles. If you own large vans or buses, seek staff members who have a commercial driving license (CDL) to transport children. It's also good practice to get routine maintenance appointments for vehicles that are being used to transport children. If you have insurance for your organization, inquire with an agent to see if you need additional insurance coverage for youth educational programs, particularly if children will be engaging in off-site activities. I also recommend conducting a Level II background screening on all teachers, staff, and regular volunteers so that you can make the best decisions about adults who will have access to and interact with children.

Community-based informal learning spaces are an important lever to the comprehensive improvement of STEM education. Churches have the capacity to help mitigate socio-educational issues if we stop turning a deaf ear. Think about the inequities that our children are faced with every day. Some of their schools are located in the most economically-challenged communities, are underresourced, and have teachers who have the least amount of experience and qualification. This is particularly true for students of color who qualify for free or reduced lunch. If we consider elementary school curriculum, reading and mathematics is probably taught every day for extended periods of time, while science and social studies are only allotted short periods of time and not taught on a daily basis.  **Commitment and consistency are critical to the development and sustenance of extraordinary programs**

Middle school becomes a critical point because this is when

students begin making connections between their personal interests, academic work, and career aptitudes. By this time, they have already decided whether or not they want to pursue the STEM trajectory, making it a critical time for them to receive positive science-learning experiences. Once students reach high school, their curricular decisions heavily influence their ability and preparedness to enter into STEM fields. This domino effect therefore makes effective STEM teaching in elementary and middle school essential to maintaining persistence in the pipeline. It further reifies the need for communities all across the nation to act in supporting schools to address such complex and systemic issues. The first step is providing authentic opportunities for children to engage in the STEM disciplines where they can see how their contributions benefit the community.

Once you address logistics and build a strong foundation, you have the capacity to facilitate extraordinary STEM programs with the spirit of excellence. There will be endless opportunities for what can be accomplished in your churches, schools, and communities. I share a testimonial from a principal who hosted I AM STEM Camp on his school campus. He shares a few examples of the STEM learning opportunities, and the impact of this work into the formal school year. Teachers benefit from the professional learning and bring lessons that they created back to their classrooms to impact more children. They also maintain their connections with community partners for sustained relationships.

Mr. Curtis Peterson, Principal of Caring and Sharing Learning School

Sometimes in life, you are presented with low hanging fruit and opportunities that are placed in your lap. I AM STEM Camp is one of those opportunities! This program has been a tremendous asset to Alachua County by educating the whole child during the summer months. Research has shown that the summer is a vital time for the continuous academic success of children, especially children of color. As the principal of a school located in an economically disadvantaged community, I understand the importance of ensuring that students are engaged during out-of-school time to prevent summer learning loss. Dr. King has done incredible work in brokering relationships and initiating partnerships so that we can offer high-quality programs to more than 300 children and their families. I AM STEM Camp exposes Pre-K through 12th grade students to careers in the STEM fields and equips them with fundamental skills that they can use to experience success in their formal schools.

Under Dr. King's leadership and vision, we offered an academically infused 8-week, full-day, summer STEM program for children in our community. Students were engaged in many activities such as visiting museums, the planetarium, and zoos, swimming lessons, tennis lessons, fishing, and even engaging in animal dissections. Students visited research laboratories in the Department of Ophthalmology and College of Veterinary Medicine, and Dr. King facilitated a Family STEM Night where parents engaged with their children in the engineering design process. Students and families alike were exposed to many opportunities that they otherwise may have never experienced.

The hands-on approach and age appropriate curriculum align with the state standards, which has assisted our school in achieving the 2017 National Blue Ribbon School Award and the 2018 National High Flying School Award. I have had the privilege of seeing the transformation of students' behavioral and academic attainment in real time. I have also witnessed students eagerly attend camp each day, and the sadness they feel as the program ends each summer. We have been intentional about infusing these inquiry-based activities into our curriculum during the formal school year and continue to leverage existing partnerships.

Our school is located across the street from the largest public housing complex in Gainesville, FL and the income level for our community is the lowest in the city. This program provided <u>access</u> *for our children to receive state-of-the-art programming. Dr. King has connected us with community partners who provide sponsorships, in-kind donations, and other supports. She also facilitates professional development with teachers and staff about how to teach in culturally relevant ways. The education sector is faced with many challenges, but this program has ensured that stimulating the minds of children in our community is not one! For this, we are grateful.*

Contemplative Questions:

1) Think about a time when your actions or words were well-intentioned, but not received in love. Why do you think this may have happened?

_____

_____

_____

What are steps that you can take to ensure alignment between your intentions and your target audience's reception?

_____

_____

_____

2) What are salient or even underlying issues that plague your community?

_____

_____

_____

What curricular ideas come to mind that can be used to promote youth awareness of and engagement in addressing local inequities?

_____

_____

_____

3) Brainstorm professional learning opportunities that would provide administrators, teachers, and staff with the necessary knowledge to facilitate high quality lessons related to the issue from Question 2.

_____

_____

_____

How can you infuse science, technology, engineering, and/or mathematics to engage youth?

_____

_____

_____

What organizations, industry partners, or even individuals would be ideal to facilitate a PD workshop?

_____

_____

_____

What off-site experiential learning opportunity can foster learning and growth related to your community issue of interest?

_____

_____

_____

PRACTICE 8

DESPISE NOT SMALL BEGINNINGS

Zechariah 4:10 – For who hath despised the day of small things?

The success of your program cannot always be measured by using numbers. Remember that little becomes much when you place it in God's hands. Your program may start off serving 20 children, but if you remain dedicated and committed, soon enough you'll have 200. In the last chapter, you read about doing everything with the spirit of excellence. Do not cut corners just because you have a small audience. An intimate setting allows you to perfect your program while building lasting relationships. Use this time to make connections and initiate partnerships that will be mutually beneficial. In seeking partnerships, share how your program will be an asset to the organization or funding agency, not just what you are expecting to receive. Look at the mission statements of nonprofits and businesses; see how their monetary donations may even satisfy one of their own organizational goals. Pray over your program and trust the process because God has an expected end in mind. You shall reap if you faint not. Start where you are, seek God, and do not be anxious for anything. Ask God for wisdom and a clear direction for how to meet the needs of the community, while also supporting the needs of the program.

There will be obstacles. You may even be in the red before you get in the green, or get a couple of L's before you can get that W. <u>Do not quit</u>! You will need to take a few risks and a couple of L's as collateral for your dream. Losses are natural. Any business owner knows that you have to invest before you can profit. Farmers can tell you that you have to plant before you can reap a harvest. Your community needs this, and the children need you! Your program will grow once you lay the foundation and plant the initial seeds. There is power in consistency, but you must persevere and remain committed! If you say that you are offering tutoring every Monday. Even if only one child shows up, tutoring needs to be held. After a while, people will know who you are, and the program will grow.

Learn how to do more with less! What in-kind donations can you secure to offset costs? What free resources are available to you? Libraries typically host free summer activities, and so include a few relevant offerings as field trips. Bowling alleys and movie theaters have good rates during the summer months and so think creatively of how you can incorporate traditional fun activities into your schedule. This is the time to work within your spheres of influence to build. Stay in budget and operate within your means so that you can provide compensation to those working the program. Do not grow faster than you're able!

In Ecclesiastes Chapter 3, the Bible talks about how life operates in seasons. No matter what season you are in, you are instructed to be content. I remember being agitated because the vision that God showed me was not my reality.

Just know that if God showed you something, He will perform it. There is a huge difference between being content and being complacent! I was satisfied with what God was doing in that season but continued shriving to perfect my craft and the program. The key is to bloom and grow where you are planted. Oftentimes, we measure our success based on the success or applause of others. We allow feelings of inadequacy to take over and delay the assignment that God has given to us. When we focus on what others are doing, we literally miss what God is trying to do through us. Focus on completing your assignment and stop spending so much time peering through your window. God will give the increase in due time.

I Corinthians 3:7-9

7 – So then neither is he that planteth any thing, neither he that watereth; but God that giveth the increase.

8 – Now he that planteth and he that watereth are one: and every man shall receive his own reward according to his own labor.

9 – For we are labourers together with God: ye are God's husbandry, ye are God's building.

Ms. Leseide Taylor, I AM STEM Parent

Choosing this summer camp 6 years ago was the best investment I made for both of my children. I AM STEM Camp has given my daughter hands-on experiences that have not only taught her essential life skills, but also how to find solutions to everyday problems. Before starting this camp my daughter Nadja was terribly afraid of public speaking. Mrs. Natalie encouraged Nadja to participate in Model United Nations and participate in the Gator MUN Conference and spend a summer at a high school institute at American University School of Communication in Washington, DC. As a result of these experiences coupled with the I AM STEM curriculum, my daughter not only speaks in front of large crowds, but she also addresses the room with power, poise, and confidence. I AM STEM Camp has also had a profound impact on my son Isaiah by fostering his love for science and technology. He has learned so much through the summer program courses that will help him tremendously in middle school, high school, college, and beyond. This camp operates under a safe, healthy, and fun environment filled with positive extracurricular activities. The teachers not only provide constant support to both of my children, but they also have a lot of resources available to help each child grow and foster their individual passions.

Trust the process because it is a journey. Proverbs 13:12 states, "Hope deferred maketh the heart sick.". The delay of what you eagerly desire can literally torment and afflict you. It is difficult to stay the course when what you're

Stay the Course. experiencing does not align with what God promised you. Sometimes you can go through the best and worst moments in your life all at the same time. Let go of what did not work or who rejected you and grow through the process. Forgive and see the greater purpose behind the pain. The famous adage that Rome wasn't built in one day still remains true. You will donate time, resources, money, and human capital. At times, it may seem like there is no return on your investment, but simply stay the course. You will not be able to see the true impact of your program right away because you have just planted the seeds. Remember, seeds take time to germinate and bring forth fruit. Water the seeds faithfully, and God will bring the increase – more families being served, robust partnerships, and even children performing better in school. The fruit of your investment will produce safe places for children during out-of-school time, break intergenerational curses of poverty, and increase the number of children graduating from college and changing the trajectory of their families. Parents may even formulate positive conceptions about school and become more involved in their children's education. Others may decide to go back to school to further their own education. Great blessings are promised to those who stay the course.

Mrs. Kimberly Welch, I AM STEM Parent

It is a pleasure to talk about I AM STEM Camp and how it has impacted my family. I noticed in elementary school, my daughter struggled in math. She would avoid math homework as it was "The Plague". Her math scores were consistently low on the FCAT/FSA each year. As a result of her struggle with math, Gabrielle began to exhibit low self-esteem and experience testing anxiety. My husband and I were at a crossroad trying to determine what road to take to get her back on track. Our prayers were answered when Dr. Natalie King and her phenomenal program helped change Gabrielle's mindset. My daughter has participated in her STEM program for approximately six years, which encourages students to be the best that they can be! It incorporates academics, cultural experiences, SAT preparation, career development, college tours, and forging friendships and bonds with peers with the same mindsets. I would recommend I AM STEM Camp to all parents who want their children to succeed.

Matthew 9:37-38
37 – Then saith he unto his disciples, The harvest truly is plenteous, but the labourers are few;
38 – Pray ye therefore the Lord of the harvest, that he will send forth labourers into his harvest.

Ms. Eleanor Mills, I AM STEM Parent

I AM STEM is the <u>BEST</u> program in the city of Gainesville. It is very structured, educational, and provides young children to teenagers with a well-rounded experience. I refer this program to parents all of the time and encourage them to register their children. I am more than 100% satisfied with the experiences that my daughter has been afforded through her participation in I AM STEM.

Don't get entangled in the intricacies that you miss the big picture!

The testimonials from parents are a gentle reminder that we cannot grow weary in well doing, because we will reap if we do not faint (Galatians 6:9). Small beginnings are simply preparing us for God's explosive blessings. Lives literally change when you stay the course, and the work becomes lighter because more individuals are vested in its success. Parents like Ms. Mills will help with recruitment, retention, and the overall sustenance of your program. Remember to keep the big picture in mind as you launch your programs, because that is what will stimulate its growth and development. I have witnessed participants like Nadja and Gabrielle transition through middle and high school and are now preparing for college. To see them gain confidence in their own skills and abilities is one of my greatest joys. Do not underestimate the work that you are doing individually, and the power of collective impact in creating spaces that allow children to thrive. Trust that God will lead the way if you focus on the big picture and stay the course.

Worker bees take on many roles in the hive which include nurturing and feeding larvae, collecting nectar and pollen, making wax, and capping the honey. They do everything but lay eggs and mate. When you are starting a program, you typically have a small core group of individuals who work together to carry out a vision. People assume multiple roles and operate outside of their comfort zones to see the vision come to fruition. If you are blessed enough to have worker bees, protect them! They will work tirelessly and do whatever needs to be done for the program to be a success. Even if they have the talent and capabilities to fill all necessary roles, provide them with balance and support. There is always so much to do in order to run a high-quality program, and when you first start out, funds may be limited. It is normal not to have all of the people in place to carry out the work, but spend time delegating tasks and ensuring that the weight of the program is distributed across stakeholders. Do not kill the worker bees because they are vital to building and sustaining your

Do not kill the worker bees.

program. Make time to show your appreciation and provide them with a helping hand.

Jeremiah 23:3-4

3 – And I will gather the remnant of my flock out of all countries whither I have driven them and will bring them again to their folds; and they shall be fruitful and increase.
4 – And I will set up shepherds over them which shall feed them: and they shall fear no more, nor be dismayed, neither shall they be lacking saith the Lord.

Be present in the moment and embrace every opportunity. When I started running STEM programs, I did not know what my ask was because we needed so many things. I operated from the program's mission and began listing out all of the barriers that were impeding us from accomplishing that mission. This is how I began to seek and build authentic partnerships.

Create authentic partnerships that lead to lasting relationships.

One issue was access to technology. We needed computers, laptops, and iPads if we were going to offer a STEM camp. I had flyers and a short elevator pitch prepared and shared it with anyone who would listen. This was not a hobby for me, it was a mandate and assignment from God. He entrusted me with the livelihood of so many children and families, and I refused to let Him down. One strategy that worked for me was being clear about the vision of the program and providing options for how individuals could partner. Invitations to collaborate ranged from asking community members to volunteer or open up their places of employment for field trips, to sponsoring an event or children to attend camp. There were so many meaningful ways that they could become involved, that was neither forced nor imposed, but rather requested and accepted. If they elected to volunteer or host a field trip, I would extend the courtesy of getting on their calendars early with a clear explanation regarding the expectations of that particular event and how they could best serve our children.

Dr. Karen Cole-Smith, Executive Director, Office of Community Outreach and East Gainesville Instruction at Santa Fe College in Gainesville, Florida

The Office of Community Outreach and East Gainesville Instruction offers many ways to help high-risk students succeed. One such example is STEM support for youth through our partnership with I AM STEM. These services and outreach efforts have helped students reach their educational and life goals. We recognize the low percentages of minorities that pursue these disciplinary areas, and through our partnership, are committed to making a positive change. As one of the partners with I AM STEM over many years, this program has definitely provided the necessary resources, contacts, workshops, and skills to ensure that we could successfully narrow the gap for those minority students who are disproportionately underserved and underrepresented in the STEM curriculum in the East Gainesville community. We have also opened up the doors to our campus for children to visit the Kika Silva Pla Planetarium and Santa Fe College Teaching Zoo every year at no cost to the program. The greatest strength of I AM STEM is their commitment to youth in our community in creating programs that are sustainable over time. I am convinced that through their efforts, and our collaboration, educational and achievement gaps have already been narrowed and students in our community will continue to experience increased success across disciplinary areas.

If you do not know where to start on your quest to developing partnerships, seek out individuals within organizations or institutions whose role is fostering community relationships and outreach efforts. They will share existing programs or opportunities that they have in place and are likely to connect you with others who can assist in moving your vision forward. Please note that the relationships you build today are always evolving, and so it's unfair to expect that they will remain the same. Be honest with your partners and have open lines of communication because as your needs and resources change, the nature of your relationship should follow suit. Partnerships must be flexible, mutualistic, and reciprocal so that all parties are benefitting while extending their resources and expertise.

This chapter culminates with a testimonial from Elder Vloedman and his wife Beverly who wanted to lead their church in local missions. They saw youth educational programs during out-of-school time as a vehicle to make a positive impact. They asked us what we needed and how they could be of service, which has been equally rewarding for them and their membership. This partnership is a prime example of how to work across denominations, generations, and races to develop strong community partnerships.

Andy and Beverly Vloedman, Elders at First Presbyterian Church (FPC), Gainesville FL

It has been our privilege to partner with I AM STEM Camp for the past 6 years. Our involvement began with a desire to do more to contribute to the lives of our neighbors. We asked the question – "How can we help?" Natalie had an answer.

Our role in the program has grown as our friendships have grown. The participation of FPC members has evolved from cooking and serving lunch for participants and their teachers on Fridays and during the last week of summer camp to hosting a weekly tutoring session at out church during the academic year. We worked with Natalie to apply for a DREAM grant for this local mission's project through our denomination. We were able to purchase technology equipment to assist with tutoring and summer programming. It is rewarding to serve as partners in a program that is changing kids' lives.

Our partnership has allowed our members a chance to participate at many levels from preparing and serving food, to tutoring students across subject areas every Monday night. We have been blessed by the relationships we have built overtime ranging from a child in the food line saying, "I remember you", or a teacher expressing their gratitude for the hot meals. One experience that resonates with me most is hearing the life story of a high school senior and assisting her with college and scholarship applications to pursue post-secondary education and her career goal. Each week, we worked together on her application materials. She became the first member of her family to attend college. Through our involvement we have experienced, in a new way, what it means to be a part of the Body of Christ.

Contemplative Questions:

1) What are some obstacles that are preventing you
   from staying the course?

   _____

   _____

   _____

   _____

   _____

2) What community groups or organizations can lead
   to more authentic partnerships to enhance and
   sustain your youth educational programs?

   _____

   _____

   _____

   _____

   _____

3) How can your place of worship provide enrichment
   and become a space for innovation?

   _____

   _____

   _____

   _____

   _____

EPILOGUE
WHO ARE YOU?

I commenced the prologue with a poem that I wrote as a 10-year old girl asking, "who am I?" As I shared seeds of wisdom on how to develop extraordinary programs, I revealed my own personal experiences and embedded testimonials from other stakeholders. This process has clarified my identity as an advocate, academic, activist, and ambassador for Christ. I no longer have to struggle with who I am and where I fit in; I am a work in progress carrying out God's divine purpose for my life.

So, who are you? What is your vision and purpose? You must have a kingdom vision in your quest to develop extraordinary youth programs where children can grow spiritually while developing 21st century skills. It is your time to take action with three easy steps – 1) write the vision; 2) speak the vision; and 3) be the vision.

TAKE ACTION #1: WRITE the Vision!

I pray that after reading through the chapters and forming responses to the contemplative questions, you can write your own vision and make it plain. The extraordinary does not happen by circumstance; it occurs by design. Now is the time to spur individual and collective action. Once you are clear about your own personal vision, bring stakeholders together and share ideas on how you can move the vision forward. Write achievable goals and brainstorm how those goals can come to fruition.

I acknowledge that I did not have the finances to engage in this work, but I learned that with obedience comes provision. God continues to blow my mind as He puts people in place to grow comprehensive and culturally-relevant programs for youth. Who knew that there was a whole book filled with knowledge and hidden truths trapped inside of me? Once I began writing the vision, I had to remember to wait for it to come to fruition because there is an appointed time. Do not become easily distracted if your programs don't grow right away. Everyone may not understand it at first, but just remain steadfast. When God speaks to your heart, listen! Do not allow fear to override what God has instructed you to do.

Stop focusing on what you don't have; shift your focus to who you have on your side.

It's okay to ask God questions if you're unsure of where to start. I had so many questions! Our candid conversations went a little like this – God, how do I write a book when I am still trying to figure it all out? Are you sure that this is what You have called me to do? I want to help others, but how do I assist them when I haven't done it in my own strength? Can you reveal to me the secret things that have allowed me to bring forth extraordinary youth programs with limited funding and resources? Give me revelatory knowledge. What words of wisdom can I share with Your people? God reassured me that I was not embarking on this journey alone. He was with me all of the time and provided the clarity and wisdom to not only birth this book, but to expand existing programs. He also gave me the infrastructure and strong foundation to accomplish my assignment; I just needed to remain a yielded vessel.

Proverbs 16:3 – Commit thy works unto the Lord, and thy thoughts shall be established.

When God gives you dreams that seem insurmountable because you do not have the tools, resources, and sometimes even the intellect to bring it forth, that's when He can shine and show forth His glory. You learn how to pray harder, fast longer, and perpetually seek His face about your next steps. Proverbs 3:5-6 instructs us to Trust in the Lord <u>at all times</u> and lean not on our own understanding. In all our ways acknowledge Him and He shall direct our paths. As I acknowledge God, He makes my path straight. You will not be able to accomplish kingdom vision and purpose on your own. When you're weak, that's when His strength is made perfect. Stay focused

God does His best work when we're yielded vessels.

on the vision that He promised unto you. God told me to write this book and I did not know where to start, how to organize it, or even how I would fill up these pages. I yielded my will and asked Him to order my steps. He gave me the chapter titles, showed me who would illustrate the book cover, and put individuals in my place to assist with final editing and publishing. He dropped the seeds in my spirit while I was driving to work, taking a shower, or even spending time in prayer. When distractions came, I held steadfast to my assignment. Instead of getting frustrated because I was unable to write every day, I stayed the course. In retrospect, I would not exchange this journey for anything because I've learned how to hear God clearly despite the noise and am finally articulating how I have navigated my Christian walk with my love for science and children!

You must write the vision in order to see the vision.

Write the vision that He has placed in your heart. As crazy as it may seem, write! All you have to do is trust God and He will give you the desires of your heart. God did not instruct us to chase after our assignment. We were instructed to seek Him, and He would order our steps. God will provide direction and give provision. I admit that a few stages in the journey were disheartening because what I was experiencing did not align with what He showed me. I saw a vision of a STEM enterprise that would change the mindsets and trajectories of those who have experienced the most oppression, while struggling with whether or not I was even worthy enough carry out such an assignment. I applied for grant funding and was denied on multiple attempts and had more doors closed in my face than I care to recall. It has been God's grace and the support from the community of believers that has helped to sustain this work. So, do not get discouraged; little becomes much when it's placed in the master's hands. God will allow you to build piece by piece and mortar by mortar to ensure that the infrastructure is sturdy enough for growth. There is always something to learn through your trials. Launching educational youth programs from the ground up has taught me how to have faith that God will make provision, but also the wisdom to complement my faith with works. It has helped me to appreciate the immense amount of commitment that is required to develop extraordinary programs so that I can, in turn, support others.

What has God placed on your heart to do? Take this time to write the vision and make it plain.

_____
_____
_____
_____
_____
_____

TAKE ACTION #2: SPEAK the Vision!

Proverbs 18:21 – Death and life are in the power of the tongue: and they that love it shall eat the fruit thereof.

As I encourage you to speak the vision, I share my own testimony of birthing I AM STEM, LLC. In 2017, I reached a crossroads and had to decide if I should focus solely on my career in the professoriate or continue this work. God showed me that I did not have to choose and gave me spiritual strategies on how I could leverage my passions to impact communities locally and globally while still fulfilling the lofty expectations of the academy. Instead of addressing year-round programs, I narrowed my focus specifically on comprehensive summer programs that leverage the arts and STEM disciplines to make curriculum come alive. The seeds were already planted and took root, reaching far beyond a single community and connecting to national narratives amongst researchers, informal/formal educators, and policymakers.

Your words have power; lift your voice and transform the narrative.

During this same time, I participated in a women's bible study at a local church using Lysa TerKeurst's book *Finding I AM*. God spoke to my spirit and kept reminding me, I AM THAT I AM. I AM was there when my journey began and continues to be with me each and every day. In my devotion, God gave me the name – I AM STEM. What's in a name? The surety of knowing who you are and whose you are. I will never lose my focus because I AM is at the core of this work. The name became even more powerful because it reified to every participant that despite underrepresentation in the STEM fields, they belong and have the capabilities to become whoever and whatever they choose. Children no longer have to be limited by their current circumstances because I AM is right there with them. They can prevail despite prejudice, discrimination, and injustice, and have spaces to problematize inequities and disparities while designing solutions to societal ills. I believe that I AM STEM Camps will build bridges and foster environments where people can build and affirm youth to realize their hopes and dreams.

I have learned the value of affirmations and have interweaved my own personal experiences and the testimonials of others throughout the book because of the power of words. We must create spaces for the voices of youth, parents, educators, faith-based leaders, administrators, and community partners to be heard. So, what widely held beliefs or misconceptions are being circulated about you, your community, and groups with which you identify? You have the power to lift your voice and transform that narrative. What words have God given you to speak? Have you opened up your mouth yet? Are you using your words to uplift your brothers, sisters, and communities?

I implore you to be careful what you say in this season. Your words should be in direct alignment with the vision that you just wrote. In times of uncertainty and disappointment, remind yourself of that vision. Remain silent if you must, but do not speak words that contradict or disaffirm the vision. In addition to speaking with your mouth, you must make a lot of noise with your actions. Your actions should align with your words; do not be lip service only.

TAKE ACTION #3: BE the Vision!

Philippians 4:13 – I can do all things through Christ who strengtheneth me.

God has given you access to everything that you need in order to carry out the vision. I learned this lesson over a series of multiple attempts to expand this transformative work. Being the vision requires you to roll up your sleeves and get in the trenches to experience the realities of the communities you are seeking to serve. As you highlight their needs, you must be just as vigilant to acknowledge the cultural resources and excellence that exists. In being the change, your mission should not be to decolonize and assimilate communities so that their livelihood and experiences mirror yours. No community should have to relinquish the essence of who they are and the authenticity of their lived experiences in order to partner with you. Remember, no funding or partnership is worth oppressing your community, or losing your voice or seat at the table. No academic agency, governmental agency, or foundation should dictate what's best for your community or carry the fate of your programs in their hands or with their dollars. They can help to inform your practices, but the decision is up to you regarding what is relevant and appropriate for the children being served. Trust and believe that once these businesses and organizations see the results of your initiatives, they will *willingly* provide financial support and engage in permissible and acceptable ways.

Break out of barriers and limitations.

Remember, God is not limited by the laws of nature or the laws of this land; He only stands by His Word. So, why are we limiting God and what we are able to accomplish in His strength? The Church can serve as the great equalizer if we change our thinking and reconceptualize our roles within communities. What are we doing to move the needle to help students develop lifelong passions for STEM learning and careers? Many individuals seek the strength of their religion or relationship with a higher being to persist within science, engineering, and mathematics; we can make room for not only spiritual guidance but become more aware of the expectations and burdens placed upon our young people and have structures in place to mitigate barriers and support them through their studies.

You can be the vision by breaking out of barriers and limitations. The testimonials presented throughout the book remind us about the potential to develop extraordinary youth programs through mutually beneficial collaborations across entities that allow individuals to operate in their strengths. There is power in breaking silos. It would be fraudulent for me to suggest that I have made to this point in my career without God's grace and the help of others. No amount of science can explain the favor that God has placed on my life. There is not enough coincidence or luck to attribute to God's goodness. Through my work, I am opening doors of opportunities for children who never considered the STEM disciplines as a viable option. Careers in STEM are more prevalent now than ever before, and we're faced with the challenge of preparing children for jobs that do not currently exist. It is so important that the Church takes a more active role in the development of the whole child. We cannot afford to be ignorant or oblivious in this season because our children need us. The Church must stop thinking so narrowly about their purpose within communities, because we will continue to see the same statistics and results if those have the knowledge, influence, and wherewithal to chip away at systemic inequities do not engage in the fight.

ENDING ON THE SAME PAGE

I close this book with a recap of the tools needed to write, speak, and be the vision. Remember, everyone has the capacity to be creative. We must envision spaces where children can exercise their **creativity** and make connections between their lived experiences and what they are being taught in school. Our places of worship should be safe spaces where children can learn about The Creator while engaging critically in difficult conversations. This divide between church and science is a social construct, because the church used to be a place to explore scholarly interests. Consider Gregor Mendel – the Father of Genetics who discovered the basic principles of heredity; he was a monk. Consider Rose Pringle, whose country town pastor introduced her to the world of education by teaching the basics of arithmetic and reading in exciting ways. Your programs must begin and end with **love**. Allow God's love to reign true as you interact with all groups of people across many walks of life. People will change once they experience the true love of Christ through your words and deeds.

When offering programs, everyone needs to be on the same page and operate in **unity** and on one accord. This means having strong leadership and robust partnerships. We must choose collaboration over competition to get more accomplished and have a greater presence in our communities. God designed us to stand out and be different. We are *in* the world but not *of* the world, and so our **light** must shine before men. Our programs should be a beacon of light where we offer something different through innovative and novel approaches. We must strive for transparency over illusions, be visible light in the community, and embrace the natural essence of who we are and were created to be. We have to exercise **stewardship** and get buy-in from the community before we can get the Benjamins. Leverage local resources and circulate money within your community before outsourcing for products and services. Your **gifts** will make room for you and bring you before great men.

Provide authentic opportunities for youth to exercise and sharpen their gifts through the arts and intellectual engagement. They can search the scriptures themselves and provide evidence to support their claims. You do not have to subscribe to traditional approaches of Sunday School or Children's Church with teachers lecturing children from a scripted curriculum. Let's make learning fun and productive by teaching them 21st century skills so that our youth can become functional citizens and adults. Let everything be done decently and in order and with the spirit of **excellence**. There are fundamentals that need to be addressed prior to launching your programs such as procedures, professional learning opportunities, and curriculum. Once logistics are ironed out, cover your program with more than prayer to minimize risks and liabilities. Finally, despise not **small beginnings**. Remember, the hardest part about starting is turning the key in the ignition. Use the first year or two to serve a small group of families; build relationships and put a strong infrastructure in place that can sustain growth.

Numbers do not give the full picture and so do not rely on numbers alone to determine the success of your programs.

Develop a solid leadership team, and recruit teachers and a few families to start the program with you. Get into the community and meet your neighbors. Who is doing business, what informal science institutions exist, what local colleges and universities are nearby? Forge relationships and begin building capacity to offer the types of opportunities that are needed at a reasonable and affordable cost. Everything is not going to work out perfectly the first few years; the key is to learn from your mistakes, listen to all stakeholders, and make the necessary adjustments.

Proverbs 11:30 – The fruit of the righteous is a tree if life; and he that winneth souls is wise.

God does not change, and His word never changes; we must change our approach because he who wins souls is wise. We're in the world and not of the world, but we have to learn the system in order to beat it. Churches have the potential to become gamechangers, but we have to get in the game first! It's not time to stand on the sidelines observing our children failing in schools or not going to college, when we can help them to progress in life, get good careers, start their own businesses, and make sound decisions. God wants to maximize and expand our impact and influence. Let us create inclusive programs that engage our children and be mentors and supporters of our next inventors and decision-makers. Sow the seeds that are embedded throughout the book, and you are sure to reap a plentiful harvest. Let's recommit ourselves to using our influence to impact the Kingdom of God.

CONNECT WITH US!

For more information about I AM STEM Camps and other STEM opportunities, please visit www.iamstemcamps.com. We would love to hear from you as you begin launching and growing your own programs. Feel free to use the hashtags #AmentoSTEM and #IAMSTEM to share photos or clips of your experiences via social media and visit www.amentostem.com or www.drnatalieking.com for additional resources and to get digital copies.

Let us put aside denominational differences and come together to promote the greater good of communities in which we live and serve.

LET THE CHURCH SAY AMEN TO STEM!

Appendix 1: Sample Calendar Overview

I AM STEM Camp Calendar
(Weeks 5-8)

WEEK 5 7/10-7/14	**10** You Be the Chemist (K-3), Science Encounter (4-Middle), Swimming (ALL)	**Tennis Lessons 11** (ALL), You Be the Chemist (4-Middle), UFCC (Middle)	**You Be the Chemist 12** (K-1), Kids in the Kitchen (K-1), Computer Coding (4-Middle), STEM GEMS Book Club (3-Middle), Swimming (ALL)	**13** Science Encounter (4-Middle), You Be the Chemist (4-Middle), UFCC (Middle)	**UF Fisheries 14** (Middle), Kids in the Kitchen (2-5), Financial Fridays with IBM (ALL)
WEEK 6 7/17-7/21	**17** Tour of the Perry Center for Emerging Technologies (Middle), Swimming (ALL)	**Tennis Lessons 18** (ALL), UFCC (Middle)	**UF Fisheries 19** (4-5), Kids in the Kitchen (K-1), STEM GEMS Book Club (3-Middle), Swimming (ALL)	**20** Science Encounter (4-Middle), UFCC (Middle)	**Computer Coding 21** (4-Middle), Kids in the Kitchen (2-5), Financial Fridays with IBM (ALL)
WEEK 7 7/24-7/28	**24** Science Encounter (4-Middle), Swimming (ALL)	**Tennis Lessons 25** (ALL), UFCC (Middle)	**Planetarium & Zoo 26** (K-3), STEM GEMS Book Club (3-Middle), Swimming (ALL)	**27** Science Encounter (4-Middle), UFCC (Middle)	**Computer Coding 28** (4-Middle), Kids in the Kitchen (2-5), Financial Fridays with IBM (ALL)
WEEK 8 7/31-8/4	**31** I AM STEM Camp Post Assessments	**August 1**	**2**	**3** I AM STEM Camp Culminating Ceremony 6:00pm-7:30pm	**4** family FUN day 9:00am-2:00pm

Appendix 2: Sample Lesson Plan Template

<<Insert Letterhead>>
<<Insert Name of the Program>>
Lesson Plans

Week (circle one)   1   2   3   4   5   6   7   8

Name: _____   Grade Level: _____

Subject _____   Topic(s) _____

Objectives:	
Standards Covered:	
Monday	Materials Needed
Tuesday	Materials Needed
Wednesday	Materials Needed
Thursday	Materials Needed
Friday	Materials Needed
Assessments:	

Lesson Plans should be completed on Fridays before the week.

Appendix 3: Sample PBL Unit Outline Pt. 1

Sample Outline - Project Based Learning Unit (Part 1)

Implementation Dates:	Name of Integrated Unit:
Teachers/Staff Collaborating:	
Community Partnerships:	

Subject:	Grade Level(s):	Standards:
1		
2		
3		
4		

List 4-6 cross-curricular vocabulary words that will be apart of the academic discourse for this unit.

Identify 1 guiding question per subject area for this integrated unit (i.e. constructive response question on common assessments)

1	
2	
3	
4	

What type of enrichment activities and projects will be included in this PBL Unit?

1	4
2	5
3	6

What guest speakers, field trips, or experiential learning opportunities will be included in this unit?

Name of Field Trip/Guest	Confirmed (Y/N)	Date of Event	Teacher/Staff in Charge
1			
2			
2			

Appendix 3: Sample PBL Unit Outline Pt. 2

Sample Outline - Project Based Learning Unit (Part 2)				
Implementation Dates:	**Name of Integrated Unit:**			
	Subject 1:	Subject 2:	Subject 3:	Subject 4:
Week 1				
Week 2				
Week 3				
Week 4				
Culminating Project or Activity				

Appendix 4: Sample Make N Take Night

■ = Geared Towards K-3
● = Geared Towards 4-Middle
♦ = Geared Towards ALL ages

Ms. DeSue	Mrs. Sheppard	Multipurpose Room
■Dancing Worms	♦Goofy Putty & Rubber Egg	Egg Drop Challenge 7:30pm
Ms. Williams	Mrs. King	Mr. Bowman
●Measurements	♦Egg Drop Design	♦Puffy Paint
Mrs. Hines	Ms. Thomas	Mrs. Lloyd
■Fry Words& Skip Counting	♦Reading Comprehension Questions	●Geometric Tents

Be sure to stop by at least two rooms in each row to get a signature/stamp.

Draw a Picture of Yourself

Favorite Subject _____

Issue Date _____

Name _____

Thank you for joining us!
We hope you enjoyed it and learned a lot
of useful activities you can share with your
children at home.

Remember to:

1. Complete and turn in your evaluation
form.

2. Wait to see which parent brought the
most visitors.

3. Turn in this passport to grab your
refreshments on your way out.

PASSPORT

MAKE N' TAKE NIGHT

Appendix 5: Sample Evaluation Form

<<Insert Letterhead>>

<<Insert Date and Location>>

<<Insert Name of Event>> Evaluation Form

Please check one of the following:

Teacher/Staff ☐   Parent/Guardian ☐   Family Member ☐   Participant ☐   Guest ☐

Is your child enrolled in <<Insert Name of the Program>>?   Yes ☐   No ☐

Please rate each statement by checking the appropriate box:

(5) Strongly Agree	(4) Agree	(3) Neutral	(2) Disagree	(1) Strongly Disagree

	(5)	(4)	(3)	2)	(1)
The teachers/staff and staff were welcoming	☐	☐	☐	☐	☐
The program met my expectations	☐	☐	☐	☐	☐
The program objectives were identified and followed	☐	☐	☐	☐	☐
The program was organized	☐	☐	☐	☐	☐
The materials distributed were useful and pertinent	☐	☐	☐	☐	☐
The teachers/staff covered the materials clearly	☐	☐	☐	☐	☐
The activities were appropriate for the occasion	☐	☐	☐	☐	☐
The teachers and staff responded well to questions	☐	☐	☐	☐	☐

	(5) Excellent	(4) Very Good	(3) Good	(2) Fair	(1) Poor
How do you rate the program overall?	☐	☐	☐	☐	☐

What session/activity did you find most useful?_____
_____

What did you like best about the program? _____
_____

What aspect(s) of the program could be improved? _____
_____
_____

What activities would you recommend for this program next year? _____
_____

Other comments? _____

Appendix 6: Sample Parent Contribution Letter

<<Insert Letterhead>>

<u>Sample Parent Contribution Letter</u>

<<Insert Date>>

Dear <<Insert Parent(s) Name>>:

Thank you for enrolling your child(ren) in <<Insert Program Name >> 2019 at <<Insert Organization Name>> in <<Insert City and State>> where they engaged in experiential learning experiences around science, technology engineering, the arts, and mathematics.

Please find enclosed a "Year-End Childcare Payment Statement" to assist you in preparing your income tax return. From January 1, 2019 to December 31, 2019, you have paid a total of $<<**Insert Amount**>> in childcare expenses for the following child(ren):

- **<<Insert Child Name>>**
- **<<Insert Child Name>>**

<< Insert Program Name >> is housed under a federally tax-exempt, 501(c)(3) organization, <<Insert Organization Name>>. You are able to claim a contribution deduction using the following EIN <u>**<<Insert EIN>>.**</u>

Registration will open on February 15th for << Insert Program Name >> *2020.* Please visit our website for more information: <<insert website>>.

Our program is not a success without your dedicated support and participation. If you have any questions or would like more information, please email <<Insert Onsite Director's Name>> at <<Insert Onsite Director's Email Address>>.

Sincerely,

<<Insert Signature of Onsite Director>>
<<Insert Name of Onsite Director, Title>>
<< Insert Program Name >>

<<Insert Signature of Executive Director>>
<<Insert Name of Executive Director, Title>>
<<Insert Organization Name>>

Appendix 7: Sample Sponsorship Request Form

<<Insert Letterhead>>

Sample Sponsorship Request Form

There are 6 main levels of sponsorship, or you may donate an amount of your choice. We are grateful for your continued support. Your name/organization will be featured on our website for any donation over $100.00. Thank you for your time and consideration.

Please mail this page to:
<<Insert Organization Name>>
Attn: <<Insert Name of Onsite Director>>
<<Insert Organization Mailing Address>>

Make check/money order payable to:
<<Insert Organization Name>>

Sponsorship Deadline:
WEDNESDAY, MAY 1st, 2019

PLEASE PRINT CLEARLY!
Name of Individual/Organization: _____
Contact Person (If different from above): _____
Phone Number: (_____) _____-_____ Email Address: _____
Mailing Address: _____

Amount Enclosed: $_____.____
Levels of Sponsorship:
_____ Diamond ($2,500+)
_____ Platinum ($1,500+)
_____ Gold ($1,000+)
_____ Silver ($500+)
_____ Bronze ($250+)
_____ Ivory ($100+)
_____ Other (please specify amount: $_____.____)

ALL DONATIONS WILL GO TOWARDS PURCHASING CURRICULUM MATERIALS AND OPERATIONS FOR OUR PROGRAM UNLESS YOU SPECIFY OTHERWISE.
☐ Check this box if you want your donation to go into our scholarship fund to assist families in need to cover registration and weekly fees.

Special Instructions or notes: _____
_____

YOU WILL RECEIVE A RECEIPT IN THE MAIL WITH 501(c)(3) INFORMATION. THANK YOU FOR GIVING

Sincerely,

<<Insert Signature of Onsite Director>>   <<Insert Signature of Executive Director>>
<<Insert Name of Onsite Director, Title>>   <<Insert Name of Executive Director, Title>>
<< Insert Program Name>>   <<Insert Organization Name>>

Appendix 8: Sample Sponsor Letter

<<Insert Letterhead>>

<<Insert Date>>

<<Insert Sponsor's Address>>

Dear <<Sponsor's Name>>:

Thank you for supporting <<Insert Program Name >> 2019 at <<Insert Organization Name>> in <<Insert City and State>> where over <<Insert Number of Children Served>> children engaged in experiential learning experiences around science, technology engineering, the arts, and mathematics. This program has proved to be successful because children leave academically ready for school with a new sense of self and exposure to careers in the STEM disciplines.

Please find enclosed an End of Year Report summarizing the types of experiences that the children were afforded this summer, evaluations of the program, financial information, testimonials, and a list of sponsors. <<Insert Program Name >> is housed under the federally tax-exempt, 501(c)(3) organization, <<Insert Organization Name>>. You are able to claim a contribution deduction using the following EIN **<<Insert Organization EIN>>** for your charitable donation to our program.

From January 1, 2019 to December 31, 2019, our records indicate that you have contributed a total of **$<<Insert Amount>>** to support the program sponsor children to attend camp.

Our program is not a success without your dedicated support and financial contribution. Please consider serving as a sponsor for I AM STEM Camp 2020. A pre-addressed envelope and Sponsorship Request Form are enclosed for your convenience. If you have any questions or would like more information, please email <<Insert Onsite Director's Name>> at <<Insert Onsite Director's Email Address>>.

You may also visit our website at any time for more information and updates about our program: <<insert website>>.

Sincerely,

<<Insert Signature of Onsite Director>>
<<Insert Name of Onsite Director, Title>>
<< Insert Program Name>>

<<Insert Signature of Executive Director>>
<<Insert Name of Onsite Director, Title>>
<<Insert Organization Name>>

REFERENCES

Bible, H. (1996). *The Holy Bible: King James Version.* Broadman & Holman Publishers.

Council of Chief State School Officers & National Governors Association Center on Best Practices. (2010). Common core state standards for English language arts and literacy in history/social science, science, and technical subjects (Appendix A). Washington, DC: Authors. Retrieved from the Common Core State Standards Initiative at www.corestandards.org/assets/Appendix_A.pdf

National Research Council. (2012). A framework for K-12 science education: Practices, crosscutting concepts, and core ideas.

NGSS Lead States. (2013). Next Generation Science Standards: For states, by states. Washington, DC: National Academies Press. www.nextgenscience.org/nextgeneration-science-standards

Southern Poverty Law Center (2016). Social justice standards: The Teaching Tolerance anti-bias framework. *Southern Poverty Law Center.*

ACKNOWLEDGEMENTS

To my husband, Tony, and sons Antonio and Angelo, thank you for your patience in my efforts to balance the demands of being a wife, mom, and professor with birthing this book. Your commitment to supporting my endeavors and always believing in me has not gone unnoticed. To Nicole, Natasha, and Chelsey, thank you for being accountability sisters and assisting with initial edits, checking on my progress, and pushing my thinking in terms of organization and development. Nadine and Clement, thank you for working with a graphic designer to bring the book cover that I envisioned to life. Ruthy, Daniel Jr., and Christina, thank you for reading chapters for clarity and accessibility to readers. Mommy, I enjoyed our conversations as you helped me to recall early memories and provided me with feedback. Dada, I appreciate your support and investment in the first 10 copies of the book.

Dr. Rose Pringle, thank you for writing the foreword and being a consistent pillar of support from my master's degree, through my doctoral dissertation, and now as an emerging scholar in the field of science education. Hotep, I'm grateful for your encouragement during the initial stages of development to publish a book. Nia Akinyemi (The Literary Revolutionary), thank you for working closely with me throughout the publishing process and helping me to establish an indisputable brand.

A special thank you to the 16 individuals who wrote testimonials that are embedded throughout the book (names and affiliations are listed immediately after the acknowledgements). Your words breathed life into me and reified my purpose for writing this book.

To all those who contributed, inspired me, believed in me, and covered me in prayer...thank you! I appreciate you more than words can express. To my family, friends, mentors, and brothers and sisters in Christ, may this book be a blessing to your homes, churches, communities, and most importantly, YOU!

Embedded in each chapter are testimonials. Thank you for your willingness to write about your personal experiences to be shared with the world.

1) Miss. Nadja Holland, *I AM STEM Participant and Intern, Gainesville, FL*

2) Ms. Eleanor Mills, *I AM STEM Parent, Gainesville, FL*

3) Ms. Leseide Taylor, *I AM STEM Parent, Gainesville, FL*

4) Mrs. Kimberly Welch, *I AM STEM Parent, Gainesville, FL*

5) Mrs. Wanda Lloyd, *I AM STEM Teacher, Gainesville FL*

6) Ms. Candace Weiss, *I AM STEM Intern, University of Florida Noyce Program, Gainesville, FL*

7) Ms. Nasseeka Denis, *I AM STEM Onsite Director at Caring and Sharing Learning School, Gainesville, FL*

8) Mr. Curtis Peterson, *Principal of Caring and Sharing Learning School, Gainesville, FL*

9) Mrs. Pamela Davis, *Executive Director of the Gainesville Housing Authority, Gainesville, FL*

10) Pastors Willie and Linda King, *Founders and Pastors of Showers of Blessings Harvest Center Inc., Gainesville, FL*

11) Dr. Natalie Marie Khoury Ridgewell, *Member, Showers of Blessings Harvest Center, Inc.*

12) Mr. Andy and Mrs. Beverly Vloedman, *Elders at First Presbyterian Church (FPC), Gainesville FL*

13) Ms. Wendy Roche, *Local Missions Coordinator of Greenhouse Church, Gainesville, FL*

14) Dr. Joanne LaFramenta, *Co-chair, Social Justice Committee, United Church of Gainesville, Gainesville, FL*

15) Dr. Karen Cole-Smith, *Executive Director, Office of Community Outreach and East Gainesville Instruction at Santa Fe College, Gainesville, FL*

ABOUT THE AUTHOR

Natalie S. King, PhD is an award-winning science educator, researcher, author, and executive director of I AM STEM, LLC. She is an assistant professor of science education in the Department of Middle and Secondary Education at Georgia State University. Her scholarly work focuses on advancing Black girls in STEM education, community-based youth programs, and the role of curriculum in fostering equity in science teaching and learning. Dr. King is passionate about preparing students to enter careers within the STEM disciplines and founded I AM STEM— an informal STEM program that provides a comprehensive curriculum embracing students' cultural experiences while preparing them to become productive and critically-conscious citizens. She challenges the capitalistic agenda for encouraging girls' involvement in STEM and reframes STEM as a mechanism to promote sisterhood and social justice. Dr. King partners with businesses, organizations, and institutions to provide children with access to comprehensive academic summer enrichment programs. She is particularly interested in dismantling divisive walls and centering faith-based institutions as an underutilized resource in communities. She believes that churches have the potential to be a driving force for STEM Education (particularly during out-of-school time) and can positively impact younger generations by promoting intergenerational relationships, civic leadership, and activism. Dr. King offers trainings and curricular support so that organizations can deliver high-quality and affordable

STEM programs to develop this generation's scientists, engineers, entrepreneurs, inventors, and mathematicians. Her work is published in the *Journal of Research in Science Teaching, Journal of Multicultural Affairs, The Science Teacher, Middle Grades Research Journal, Teaching and Teacher Education*, and the *Urban Education Research and Policy Annuals*.